# The Cross Leads Home

## Amir C. Parshad

ISBN
978-1-956161-80-9 (Paperback)
978-1-956161-79-3 (eBook)

I want to thank Rev. George A. Desjardins, formerly Director of the 100 Huntley Street in Ottawa Prayer Center for his help and kindred spirit. My many thanks to Brett Gorman for his great help on the journey of bringing this book to print and assisting with computer set up, and to Noel Christopher Parshad for help in its publication. My thanks to Alisha Parshad for kindly designing the front cover.

I thank my Lord Jesus for all my children, siblings and others who walk with Him. I thank God for all who will be blessed by reading this book.

In the cross of Christ our Lord
Be our glory forever;
Lead us in love with God and each other,
One Church on earth as
It is in heaven.

*In loving memory of my wife,*
*Roseline Parshad*

# Contents

# Why Love?

**Love** is the greatest power that is greater than any other power that ever existed or will exist. God is love, and love originated from God. Everything that He has created is His loving handiwork both on this earth and in heavens God indeed had made man in His own image and loved them so much that He placed them in the Garden of Eden. And when Jesus came, the Bible says: *God so loved the world, that he gave his only begotten Son, that whosoever believeth in him should not perish, but have everlasting life* (John 3:16). The Apostle Paul, though once an enemy of the followers of Jesus Christ, when he heard Jesus asking him: "Saul, Saul, "why persecutest thou me? (Acts 9:4) , love for the world became his heartbeat and he wrote: *And now abideth faith, hope, love, these three; but the greatest of these is love* (1 Corjnthianjs 13:13).

The life indeed is beautiful because everything that exists is the product of God's love. But when mankind lost the love of God and decided to go their own way, their love for each other also diminished considerably. Beside losing their joy of living comfortably, it also caused diversity among them. Thus, when mankind lost their love for God, the devil opened wide death's door.

Jesus came to this earth for He had seen that the whole world was lying in darkness of sin, and this darkness had made them to forget God who had made them and surrounded them with His love and intended them to live in the Garden of Eden in perfect peace, and not in any slavery. But the enemy had cunningly come, tempted them and made their love for each other also to diminish. He also considerably succeeded to draw them away from God. Now in the slavery of sin and absence of any help from

1

anywhere, only God was their source of recovery. Therefore, when Jesus came, He told them: *I am come that they might have life, and that they have it more abundantly* (John 10:10). Thus, Jesus came to restore mankind of all that which was lost. He restored their fellowship with God though He had to pay a great price by laying His own life on the cross, He earnestly desired them to be one with Him and with each other; but we still ended with more divisions among ourselves as diversity also flourished. The very Church is split up as denominations sprang up in every quarter. Because the gap between God and man had become so big, Jesus had said: *the Son of man is come to save that which was lost* (Matthew 18:11). Therefore, with a heavy heart, Jesus had said: *how often would I have gathered thy children together, even as a hen gathereth her chickens under her wings, and ye would not! Behold, your house is left unto you desolate. For I say unto you, Ye shall not see me henceforth, till ye shall say, Blessed is he that cometh in the name of the Lord* (Matthew 23:37-39).

Jesus came and made it possible for us to know Him personally. He also paved the way for us to take us back to our original abode in Paradise and live in peace and love with each other. Christ's mission was to bring back to mankind the love that was lost when mankind had forgotten God. Now to keep us safe from the enemy, He intends to keep us with Himself and also safe under His wings.

The Church is the planting of His love, and she needs His protection. Therefore, we ought to come and join ourselves with Him. As we do this, the joy of His salvation descends upon us and we are restored. This love breaks all barriers because it was His love that brings us back and gives us peace. For when He died on the cross, even the death could not hold His love for mankind. And He rose again so that in Him we may become His joy. Now He gives us the joy of living and rejoicing with each other, for it gives Him pleasure to see when we all unite with Him.

When He came to meet His disciples at His resurrection, He spoke to them: *Peace be unto you* (Luke 24:36). This peace is so great that it is ever eager to restore the whole world and save them from the hand of the enemy. Therefore, He still tenderly invites all mankind saying: *come unto me, all ye that labour and are heavy laden, and I will give you rest* (Matthew 11:28). And at the time of His ascension to heaven, He asked Peter, (and so He asks us): *lovest thou me ... Feed my* lambs (John 21:15). He repeated it three times. When He asked: 'do you love me', He is calling us to come and experience His love for it makes us His own again. This acknowledgment then calls us to feed His sheep or lambs. Leading sheep or lambs is a very loving act. For loving sheep/lambs would naturally lead us to feed His sheep, the mankind, with His messages of love. It also woos those who are lost or backslidden, to come back home.

But we still did not believe Him and went our own ways and are divided into hundreds of churches. In this divide, we have become busy in building our own lives, and many have built empires. We have forgotten that without God the snares of the enemy will make us more desolate. But He is able to deliver us from yet many of unseen and hidden attacks of the enemy. God had planned that we all be safe by being under His wings, because under His wings we are not only safe but are one enjoying warmth of His love too; Therefore Jesus had prayed: *That they all may be one* (John 17:21). In unity there is power and it is a source of blessing from above. But we have gone so far apart from Him and from each other, that it is only God who can restore our scatter structures. Therefore, Jesus has said: *I am the way* (John 14:6). God is love and He longs to see us glorified like Him for we are made in the image of God. Jesus has always done great things for us, now it is our turn to **let Jesus be Jesus** in all our coming and going. The end time is approaching and we have an appointment with God; therefore, there is urgency to do what Jesus says and let Him bring end-time victories in His Church. For when we love Him, loving our fellow beings, irrespective of who they are, will naturally be a great joy. When the love will come and bind us to Him and with each other, we will also know that we are changed from glory to glory. Unbelief started in the Garden of Eden, but at the Cross we were united again with Him and are destined to go back to the Garden of Eden. This is that unity which will bring heaven to earth. And unity with our fellow brothers and sisters will be so precious that loving those who hated us will a sheer joy; as was the unity of the repenting criminal who was at the cross with Jesus and Jesus took him with Him to Paradise. Jesus has commanded us: *love one another, even as I have loved you* (John 13:34).

The cross of Jesus was made of two pieces of wood. When these two pieces were joined together, we, who live on this earth, were also joined to our maker and become one. Therefore, we are one body and also are called His children. And in resurrection we became 'the children of resurrection'. It seems that the vertical piece of the cross represents Jesus and the horizontal was for mankind that represents the one solid Church. Jesus had said: *If any man will come after me, let him deny himself, and take up his cross, and follow me* (Matthew 16:24). We all, as one unit, have to carry our piece of the cross, as one solid Church. It was all accomplished and sealed by His resurrection in the presence of heaven and earth. Since then, the cross has become the banner of victory for us too. This banner alone will usher us to march into His glory for it binds the earthly to the eternal and makes the sinners, saints. We are one with Jesus because of the Cross, because when we come to Jesus, the Bible says: *Blessed is he that cometh in the name of the Lord* (Matthew 23:39). What a joy it will be when we all get to heaven, and will be filled with love overflowing for we will be one with Him, and in unison will be singing songs of praise and love for our Victor. And when the life is over on this earth, we could hear Him saying: *Well done, good and faithful servant; thou hast been faithful over a few things, I will make thee ruler over many things: enter thou into the joy of thy lord* (Matthew 25:23). The purpose of life will then be gloriously understood how wise it was to bind each one of us with Jesus and also with each other in chords of love which cannot be broken. Therefore,

> In the Cross, In the Cross,
>> Be our glory ever
> Bind us to each other and to You
>> One Church on earth as it is in heaven.

# Vision of the Covenant

It was the night of December 30, 1996 in Ottawa, Canada that I remember like it was yesterday. Snow had already covered this land from sea to sea. With Christmas festivities over, thoughts turned to the New Year. There was a news report that caught my attention. On the Eiffel Tower in Paris, amidst the glittering festive lights of the season the number of days left to usher in the year 2000 was flashing brilliantly.

I had a very gracious vision in my dream. Its importance seemed of great significance. In it, I was instructed to follow a certain direction. A time was also specified for its implementation. The dream unfolded as follows:

There was a narrow country road and all around it was beautiful greenery. On this road, I was heading north on my bicycle. Suddenly, the road became wide and well paved. As soon as it became wide, I was going down a hill. I had hardly covered a distance of twenty or thirty feet on this slope when I discovered that there was no road ahead, but a great canyon. Along the road there was no warning posted. Where the road ended there was no barrier. I suddenly stopped my bicycle by turning its front wheel to the left.

Dismounting from the bicycle, I walked to the end of the road and looked below. There was a drop of about 2,000 feet. At the bottom, it looked like an enormous dry riverbed with large rocks spread all over. As I stood observing the drop, I saw a train at the bottom of the canyon moving east. It looked so small that it seemed like a toy train. I was very angry that there was no warning posted along the road. Anybody could have fallen there and died instantly.

5

As I returned from the edge, moving in the southern direction, immediately on my right hand, which would be the west side of the road, I observed a slightly elevated ground. There were beautiful bushes and in the background were beautiful green trees.

A man in greenish apparel was standing there. His clothes were like the clothing of John the Baptist as is seen in paintings. My spirit witnessed to me that he was the greatest friend that I could ever have. It was my Jesus whom I met. He was facing east as I approached him. In front of him, he had two wooden logs; each of them was about six feet long and about six to seven inches in diameter.

He said to me that one log was his and the other was mine. He then said: "Let us put a knot to these." I was surprised as to how a log can be tied to another in a knot. He put forth his right hand and from one end of his log he took about one fourth of the thickness of the log and pulled it to its middle. It still remained attached to his log. I did the same with my log and pulled the same thickness out half of the way with great ease with my right hand. Now both the pulled ends were meeting in the center as the two logs lay on the ground. Then He said: "Let us put a knot to these." I thought that pulling it was easy, but how can wood be joined to another wood in a simple knot. However, at His saying, when we started putting a knot to these, it was so easy as one knots a rope. We put two knots to these two logs.

After this, He directed me to another paved road that was on his right, just a few feet away leading toward west. He said to me that on it at the eighth mile, I should turn right. I, somehow, understood in my spirit that, when I turn right on this road that on its eighth mile this road will take me to the mountains, possibly the Himalayan mountains since the entire scene was familiar to me from my childhood. Now on this road I was driving a car. As I proceeded at His bidding, this road in the valley was surrounded with green forests and the scene was similar to that on the Trans-Canada Highway.

Then I considered that the odometer in my car indicated the distance in kilometers. How would I then know when I have to take a right turn at the eighth mile? Previously I had a car that showed the distance in miles and this was the car that I was driving in this dream.

This was the end of the vision I had in my dream.

I realized that this vision was of great importance and significance. Analyzing it became a serious matter. I found that the early part of the dream—coming on a narrow road and then the road becoming wide all of a sudden—was the picture of my life. About the road becoming wide, the Bible says: *wide is the gate, and broad is the way, that leadeth to destruction* (Matthew 7:13). If I had continued on that road which had become wide, I would have fallen in the canyon of my life and died.

However, stopping the bicycle before reaching the edge of the drop of the canyon probably meant that it was a turning point in my life. If I had continued, I would have plunged into a deep gorge from which there was no return.

Getting down from the bicycle and viewing the danger ahead meant taking account of where I was heading. In my dream I stopped, took account of where I would have ended, made a 180-degree turn and beheld that on my right my greatest friend was standing. It was only when I turned around to face the other way that I met Him.

We also have to turn from our ways and meet our greatest friend, Jesus, who is always at our right hand (Psalm 16:8), as I saw Him.

I reflected on the dream and discussed it with a few friends and we concluded that the man in my dream was Jesus Himself. He is indeed our greatest friend. It was He who had brought the two pieces of wood to join together. One log belonged to Jesus and the other to me. He suggested that these two logs be joined together. Though this task seemed impossible, I knew that everything is possible with God.

The Cross on which Jesus died was also made up of two logs. I then realized that one log surely represented mankind. The purpose of the two logs became clear because the sole purpose of the Cross is to join mankind with God. It was at the cross that man was reconciled to God. He pulled a piece of His log for me first. After it, I pulled a piece from my log too. It is always God who takes the initiative and puts us on the right track.

He has taken the initiative. We have to do our part. When we are obedient and do our part, we see that things which seem impossible become so easy, even knotting two logs together. Things which we could never do happen because we are united with Jesus.

When both the logs are joined in a knot, it becomes one unit. Thus, His log and our log form a cross. That is precisely the meaning of the

Cross. Because of the Cross, we are united to Him. When we find ourselves on the cross too, the meaning of the Cross becomes so clear because it binds us together with eternal love which previously seemed impossible to the human mind.

The two logs joined together in a double knot represent a covenant which I would like to call, 'Covenant of Wood.' Binding these pieces together with each other was His idea and is significant.

After I, a member of the human race, was bound to Him with a covenant, I was instructed to take the road on His right. It meant that I was to keep to the truth.

Then turning to the right at the eighth mile most possibly represented the eighth day, eighth week or eighth month or eighth year or the eightieth year of my life. At which time I was instructed to make a right turn. The significance of this seems to be that at that time I was to do what my greatest friend had in mind for me to do. That road, or action, was to take me to the mountains, which usually signifies the glory of God. Christian friends also felt that the eighth mile most likely was the eighth month which would be the end of August, 1997.

I watched carefully for things to happen on the eighth day, then on the eighth week, and finally on the eighth month. The month of August ended and I was still wondering about the significance of this dream. The time was most possibly right, and I was in earnest to turn right by taking the right step, whatever it was.

Prior to this time for a few months my spirit had been disturbed over affairs in churches, but I had not done anything. To my amazement, and not by my design, by the end of August, I had started jotting down these thoughts which were scattered and varied. Thoughts would flood my empty mind like a river. I hastened to write them down as fast as I could. However, I was still waiting as to when I had to turn to the right at the eighth mile.

During this time, a friend to whom I had told the dream was asking me if anything had happened. As we were talking about the two logs, I suddenly realized in my spirit the meaning of knotting these two logs which in the natural is impossible. It was as though the Spirit of God had opened a new vista for understanding this mystery. I jumped up and told this friend something like this: "Paper is made out of wood, or logs. The Lord is revealing that in paper form, logs can be combined. They can be bound together. I must bind all these thoughts in a book form." To me the mystery was solved. The Lord wanted this message to go in the form of a book, which I had, quite unawares; already started writing and the Lord also had already started dictating. The writing of this book had started right on time.

I am only a servant of the Lord. As a servant, I have to do what my greatest friend, Jesus, has instructed me. I am bound to Him with the 'Covenant of Wood.' Since I am accountable to Him, this is all the more reason why I should be found faithful. I also pray that, since we all will be accountable to Him, we all may be found faithful. I can say with Paul: *necessity is laid upon me; yea, woe is unto me, if I preach not the gospel* (1 Corinthians 9:16).

# Glory of Visiting the Cemetery

Something extraordinary was going to happen. At creation, *the earth was without form, and void; and darkness was upon the face of the deep. And the Spirit of God moved upon the face of the waters, And God said, Let there is light; and there was light* (Genesis 1:2-3). This was the event of the first day of creation.

On another occasion, darkness had covered the earth for three hours. But this darkness was also going to vanish as divine light and life eternal were going to be the song in the resurrection era. For the heavenly messengers had come to declare that 'He is risen' 'See He is not here.' Now in this light, darkness was replaced because of God's great love for mankind. Thus, once again divine light was seen. Therefore, for the dwellers of this age, Jesus had said "ye are the light of the world."

It was the first day of the week and Jesus came walking on the wings of resurrection. At creation the first thing that was created was light and life came into being. Now with Christ's resurrection, redemption and new life dawned. The resurrection had broken down the chains of darkness and sin.

The first day of the week had emerged and some women, who were present at the hill called Calvary, had hurried early in the morning to the tomb where Jesus' body was laid. As they were looking for the body of Jesus to anoint Him, glorious Jesus met them alive. He was no more in grave clothes for these were left in the tomb. What an awesome moment it was they saw - the resurrected Christ - the first fruit of them that slept. Now the carnal could hope to be immortal. Now, because of our relationship with Him, we have our Savior who lives, we shall live also. Children of resurrection have this relationship with Him in both life and in death.

That same day there was another group of believers. They were in a room with doors shut. The comfort and safety of home could not take their fear away. It is strange that there was fear in those at home, but in those who had gone to the tomb divine love and divine fear brought them into the glory of resurrection. They thus became a deterrent to the enemy.

The Bible tells us - *God hath not given us the spirit of fear; but of power, and of love, and of a sound mind* (2 Timothy 1:7). There is a 'spirit of fear' which is demonic. But: *fear of the Lord is the beginning of wisdom* (Psalm 111:10). This gives us power, love and a sound mind. That is why Jesus said: *Fear Him which after He hath killed, hath power to cast into hell: yes, I say unto you, Fear Him* (Luke 12:5). But the women and the two disciples who went to the tomb had wrapped themselves in love for Jesus and chose of their free will to go where He was laid. To dispel evil fear, the angels told them: *"Fear not"*. With Jesus there is no fear, in this life or in the life to come.

But others disciples had the doors shut because of fear of life. When we are not seeking God, the spirit of fear seeks us. The spirit of fear is upon many Christians and Christian leaders. Their fear is about their own lives, their ministry and their prestigious positions.

There is a fear that leads us to the truth and there is also the spirit of fear which leads us away from the truth. Thomas had heard from his fellow disciples, but he would not believe that Jesus had risen from the dead. The same can be said about many Christians and their leaders. They have been too comfortable just knowing a little about Jesus and not coming to the point of meeting Him personally in His resurrection. It seems, some have no time to go to the cemetery and meet Him with all their heart. He still appears to us in His infinite love, and we with our analytical mind, like Thomas, do not believe that He is alive and holds the keys of abundant life.

Our higher learning and analytical mind often do not allow us to believe such witnesses. However, those who went to the place where He was laid saw the risen Christ. They saw the tomb empty and clothes lying in an orderly fashion. Some held to His feet. Then they ran to tell the disciples the greatest news ever. And Jesus talked to them. When they again saw Him in His resurrection, it was joy full of glory.

Before seeing the glory of resurrection, it was necessary for them to go to the cemetery. And those who went and saw His awesome resurrection were changed from glory into glory. They had learned so much during the three years of their studying with Jesus, but only going to the cemetery did they understand the real meaning of their ministry. Thomas, a disciple of the Lord, had not gone to the cemetery. Therefore, he was doubtful. However, Jesus came to him when he was sitting with a mixed group—some believing His resurrection, others still doubting. He came to Thomas and conversed with him. Thomas then discovered that He was Jesus indeed resurrected and said: *My Lord and my God* (John 20:28). It was as if he himself had gone to the cemetery and seen all that his fellow disciples had told him.

In both these cases—disciples going to the cemetery and others who believed when the time came—we see a strange phenomenon. The time of believing came upon them with power and awe. These disciples died to their earthly way of thinking. Only when they died to their thinking did they rise up and became children of resurrection. Like Thomas, many of us have doubts that have barred us from seeing the truth. Let us all go to the cemetery and see Him for ourselves, leaving all doubts and thinking behind. Then come out with Christ wearing beautiful robes of His resurrection.

Resurrection comes only when death has taken place. But the glory of resurrection takes place on those who seek Him and have picked up their cross on which Jesus had bound them. Jesus in His resurrection was seen only by His own. And to His own he had invited to see Him in Galilee. Then their lives become a deterrent to the devil and his horde. Real belief comes when all doubts are replaced by meeting Him. The Bible says: *seeing that ye have put off the old man with his deeds; And have put on the new man, which is renewed in knowledge after the image of him that created him* (Colossians 3:9-10). Yes, when we put the old man into the cemetery and put on the resurrection of Christ, we must be very diligent to keep wearing these clothes of resurrected belief.

Normally, at the cemetery, realization comes that death is the end of all life on earth. Jesus died but His resurrection brought the greatest news that - because He lives, we shall live too. The disciples still witness that only in a cemetery does resurrection take place. However, death must precede resurrection. It is time for all to go to the cemetery because before we proclaim the resurrection of our Lord, we also must rise up with Him.

Like Jesus, we must also leave our grave clothes in the tomb. Grave clothes are the covering that we had upon us when we were lying dormant in our old life. However, when we have experienced our resurrection, we can also witness to this world like the first disciples did. When our old self is buried and we have become alive in Jesus, then, having the power of His resurrection in us, we shall be able to do what Jesus wants us to do in this world, even move the mountains in His name.

*And when he had called unto him his twelve disciples, he gave them power against unclean spirits, to cast them out, and to heal all manner of sickness and all manner of disease* (Matthew 10:1). When Jesus sent them, these disciples had graduated from the Master's school of learning, but they experienced a great difference in their lives having come to the tomb. They met Him who knows what is beyond the grave. They had previously heard Him saying: *I am the resurrection* (John 11:25), but when they saw Him again, they became: *children of the resurrection* (Luke 20:36).

These children of resurrection now had a new message that, in Christ: *Death is swallowed up in victory* (1 Corinthians 15:54). Believers, it is time to go and follow Jesus all the way for Jesus has bound us on His cross with unparalleled love.

# The Bride

The Church, the bride of Jesus Christ and is the glory of God. About her, Jesus said: *I will build my church; and the gates of hell shall not prevail against it* (Matthew 16:18). On earth, she has the power to move the mountains. In the name of her Master, Jesus, she wields power upon all the demonic forces. The Church is an organism. Therefore, she has the capability of reproducing children for the kingdom of God. Angelic beings minister to her and she always has the company of her Master (Matthew 28:20). The power and glory ascribed to her are beyond comprehension. She is also the honored servant of The God Most High.

When the Church is aware of her status, she is more than a conqueror. In every battle, victory is hers through her Master. During the ministry of her Master on this earth, demons were expelled, the sick were healed, the dead were raised, the kingdom of heaven was preached and sinners were redeemed. The Gospel declares that Jesus came: *To give light to them that sit in darkness and in the shadow of death, to guide our feet into the way of peace* (Luke 1:79). The Church was also told that she would do greater works (John 14:12). When she realized this truth, glory filled the hearts of everyone who came in contact with her wherever she went. People were added to the Church every day. She grew enormously and the world witnessed revivals. There was rejoicing in heaven also that sinners were given the robes of salvation and righteousness.

However, the Church on earth has not always been as she should be. She has often been tossed to and fro. The enemy has incessantly beaten her with floods of animosity and high winds of hatred. History has not hidden these facts. At every attack, it seemed, the Church was disillusioned. A few that survived these assaults brightened the world with the Gospel of Jesus Christ, because the light and life in them was unquenchable.

Many victims of such assaults, who were not faithful to the Master, found shelter under denominational umbrellas. Many of these denominations had sprung up because of the attractiveness of worldly security and their lukewarm faith. Further splits within these denominations were caused as diverse new ideologies were introduced to keep these churches aligned with social and political changes. Instead of being the light in this dark world, darkness was brought into these churches as we slowly stepped into the Dark Ages.

Jesus, in His high priestly prayer, had prayed: *That they all may be one; as thou, Father, art in me, and I in thee, that they also may be one in us* (John 17:21). Instead of unity, denominations started springing. They forgot to look within and lost sight of their vocation. Instead of being one in the Lord, their human wisdom dictated them to go for worldly honors and glory. Education and scholarship also gave them incentives to grope for new ideologies. Philosophy and psychology made inroads into the churches. Under the banner of advancement, the counsel of men replaced the counsel of God. Under the banner of education, the Word of God was doubted and debated by scholars. Denominational rivalry dominated as efforts were geared to attracting more members into the competing denominations than to Christ.

Superiority complex replaced Christ's standard of considering others better. Aristocracy became the norm in these churches rather than servanthood. Under the guise that God is love, the holy fear of God has been neglected. The Bible took a back seat and formalism made great stride. In the absence of right priorities, people remained spiritually hungry. Although the church hierarchy knew that God must be acknowledged in every phase of worship, they found it difficult to lead their congregations in God's way because they themselves had not known God. Without knowing God personally, they found it difficult to pray effectively. Thus, Prayer Books were introduced so that, in the absence of praying in the spirit, they could use prayer texts. This was the intellectual way of saying to the Holy Spirit, "See, how fine are our prayers which we have set out." We indeed have grieved the Holy Spirit greatly. How can a blind person lead the blind?

Most denominations paid little interest to the Great Commission. As the Spirit of God was grieved, unification in the churches gave way to diversification. New ideologies had no restraining power in them. Therefore, there were further splits within these denominations. Instead of real love, humbleness before God and the brotherly love, there emerged superiority. Religious institutions got puffed up with pride as the elite started coming from their denominational Bible schools and seminaries. Religious doctrines became paramount and thus spirituality was clothed in new dogmas. The pseudo bride that emerged became clothed with education, formalism and church doctrines. She became very proud.

We thank God that the real bride was still adorned with fine jewels of heaven throughout this time. People like Martin Luther, John Wesley, John Newton, Sadhu Sunder Singh, Watchman Nee, and scores throughout the centuries made tremendous strides. People like the Plymouth Brethren fled to the New World and the Bible was translated into many languages for the Holy Spirit was still searching for the lost.

In God's presence, pride of this world, knowledge, education and our great names, must not boast. What God has designed will bear fruit. If education does not bear fruit, we should change our systems of learning and begin at the feet of Jesus. Was it not Mary who sought to listen to Jesus at his feet? Was Martha not told: *one thing is needful: and Mary hath chosen that good part, which shall not be taken away from her* (Luke 10:42)? Only at Jesus' feet can we find solace for our mind, soul and spirit. Let us all learn from the Holy Spirit who always teaches us all about Jesus. Paul had earlier studied under Gamaliel, probably the greatest academic institute of his time. Like Paul, all our previous learning as he had before he met Jesus, must be replaced with the glory of God. We shall then become spiritually wise and be able to lead the sin-driven world to Jesus who has the answer to all our problems. He is the Alpha and Omega.

Christ's bride has got to be spotless and holy. If we are not spotless, whose bride are we going to be? Now is the time to seek the Lord. Ask Him to cleanse each one of us and make us His spotless glorious Church and do what He wants us to do. We all need to be bound with Jesus at the Cross.

# The Church Must Rise and Shine

Jesus Christ has laid the foundation of the Church. She is the glory of God and her building is magnificent. But, amidst its many triumphs, it has suffered both externally and internally through the ages. It has been a battlefield in this world as spiritual and physical wars are waged against it continuously. When we have tried to be the light in this world, we seem to be groping to find its glory. We know that we have been fragmented into denominations and sectors. Yet the Church has endured the times because of its truth, the simple way, the life that it gives and its author. Surely, Jesus said: *and upon this rock I will build my Church, and the gates of hell shall not prevail against it* (Matthew 16:18).

Moved by this, the writer purposed to search the Scriptures in seeking God's plan to bring light to the things that we have paid little attention so that His glory might return in the Church. It is a solemn desire expressed in the Scriptures that our faith may arise to the heights that God would be pleased and His glory might appear upon His people. Jesus prayed for the Church that they all may be one in Him (John 17:21). Therefore, in union with Him, we must rekindle the lamp that has gone so dim.

By observation, we see that Christians fall into three categories. (a) There are some who call themselves Christians but do not believe in God. (b) There are those who believe in God but doubt that He is 'Almighty and powerful'. (c) Many believe that God is Almighty, has saving power to heal and save. The simple truth is that God has a great interest in everyone.

Jesus came from heaven to this earth to show us the way to life eternal. When He said in John 10:10, that they may have it (life) more abundantly, His desire was that we might be His delight in this world and show forth His glory and power. Thus, He said: *let your light so shine before men that they may see your good works and glorify your Father in heaven* (Matthew 5:16).

## Wisdom's Plan

God, who made us, has also created the heavens and the earth, the galaxies and all that exists and He looks after them all. He has given life and strength to all of His creation. He even teaches newborn babies and gives them wisdom to know the new world they have just stepped into. Thus, to each one of us, He has endowed wisdom to go through all life's trials and struggles.

## Life's Complexities

We often meet situations in life, which are quite complex. Simple problems we handle ourselves. For more difficult ones, we look to others, and also then to the wisdom of the world. Little do we consider that God is the source of all wisdom and knowledge. King David knew that God was keen to help and guide us all. He simply followed God's plans in all his circumstances. For this, he is known as the best king that man has known. For his simple trust in God, God also trusted him and made him great among the kings of the world. Little do we understand that the Spirit of God longs to guide us always even when our paths may be slippery. In fact, He wants to lead us in green pastures. Look, He says: *call upon me in the day of trouble: I will deliver thee* (Ps 50:15).

## Jesus is the Answer

Jesus passionately said: *Come unto me **all ye*** (Matthew 11:28), He knew that there is no one who can help as He can – not even earthly parents. Our earthly fathers are not perfect, and they are here for a while. But our heavenly Father never fails. He treats us better than our earthly fathers. For this reason, He said: *for one is your Father, which is in heaven. Neither be ye called masters: for one is your Master, even Christ* (Matthew 23:9-10). Indeed, there is no man who can guide like Jesus does, for He is all knowing. Neither can any nurture as He does for His resources are infinite. Who can understand His power, knowledge and wisdom? He is our real teacher for all His ways are much higher. None of us with all the knowledge that we have can calm the roaring sea in our lives or give rest to all our fears. He who has given us life knows all that we ever need. Our knowledge is too little to replace His compassionate resources.

## Scriptures Speak

Much learning has caused diverse philosophies and theologies to flourish and we have become target of these. The Scriptures warn us: *Beloved, believe not every spirit, but try the spirits…because many false prophets are gone out into the world* (1 John 4:1). Therefore, Jesus said: *It is written in the prophets, 'And they shall be all taught of God. Every man therefore that hath heard, and hath learned of the Father, cometh unto me.* (John 6:45). He also said: *I am the way, the truth, and the life. No man cometh unto the Father but by me* (John 14:6). So, we should search the Scriptures as the Christians in Berea searched the scriptures daily, *whether those things were so* (Acts 17:11), and are example to us. Our learning from Him enables us to grasp the eternal sources.

## Trust that Excels

It is beautifully stated: *they that wait upon the Lord shall renew their strength; they shall mount up with wings as eagles, they shall run, and not be weary; and they shall walk, and not faint* (Isaiah 40:30). Waiting upon the Lord only makes us to reach heights unheard of and is the source of all strength. It is in that strength that we can walk and run tirelessly to tell others the Good News. Then the Lord will make us strong both before men and God.

Excellent examples are given in the Bible of saints who trusted God despite all odds and at all cost as the following examples illustrate -

**Job** was attacked with umpteen calamities but he said: *though after my skin worms destroy this body, yet in my flesh shall I see God* (Job 19:26). He found himself wrapped in the heart of God as the over whelming power engulfed him and restored to him twice as much as he had before.

**Daniel**'s unwavering trust in God brought awe upon the hungry lions for they treated him as their guest. They did not harm him. Seeing God's help and power, King Darius could not hold his peace. He thus wrote to all in his great empire what he saw and proclaimed to: *...fear before the God of Daniel; for he is the living God, and steadfast forever, and his kingdom that which shall not be destroyed, and his dominion shall be even unto the end* (Daniel 6:26). This acclamation also makes us to realize that God's resources are infinite in all His creation, and our life and security are also in Him.

**Shadrach, Meshach and Abed-nego** – God greatly honored them by walking with them in the fiery furnace that was made seven times hotter. Even the fire and the furnace lose all their natural ability in God's presence when God is with His heroes. A closer walk with God always subsides all fear and faith shine gloriously. His love is displayed to His children in all their fiery furnaces.

**Noah** - for 120 years faithfully built the ark at God's command. It was to sustain life on this earth. As the cargo stepped into the boat for a new world, it pleased God to lift them higher and higher. Noah's obedience alone saved life on earth that followed the deluge. We thank you, Noah, that you trusted God whole heartedly. We all are alive today because of his unwavering faith and are blessed as the life continues.

**Enoch, Abraham and innumerable others** are known for their lofty trust in God. Their walk was beautiful for they walked with God with all their heart. Therefore, they became the delight of the Almighty for they saw that God's hand was upon them. The blessings they received are still shared by many through the ages. The secret of being the heroes of faith is to have complete trust in God alone in obeying.

All these and many more were men of faith though they went through life's many trials. Some became fools for God, but because they were taught by God, they walked in victory. They heard God and He became their salvation and pride. They had the faith that comes by hearing ... the Word of God (Romans 10:17). They knew that faith cannot be diluted. Faith is magnificent and full of glory and no earthly wisdom can dim its light.

## An Excellent Friend and Teacher

A true friend is one who always has his friend's best interest at heart. This is love that the very sound of his friend is so welcome. Jesus has become our friend - there is no friend like Him. Like a friend, He comes to us to help us, and lovingly teaches, or tells us all things that are good. The sweet Psalmist says: *O God, thou hast taught me from my youth* (Psalm 71:17). And because we are His children, God loves to teach us. He has made us to become like Him and have His wisdom and knowledge. Therefore, whatever He says, we should hear attentively for it will be for our good. He speaks to us through His Word, Himself and through our own heart. If we would not listen to Him, we are leaning on our own understanding or our earthly abilities. It is then that our pride overtakes us and our short achievements bereave us of His many blessings. From the beginning God has taught man how to live in this world so that we might learn we are His children. He did so by sending the law and His prophets, and then His Son Jesus. And our Friend pours out his Spirit upon us. Apostle Paul affirms: "the Spirit also helpeth our infirmities" (Romans 8:26). He simply wants us to be His light in this world so that this world may know that we are His children, His friends and taught by Him. It is God who guides us all the way to eternity.

To help us, our Friend Jesus says: *I am come that they* (we) *might have life, and that they might have it more abundantly* (John 10:10). By having a more abundant life, we are called: *a chosen generation, a royal priesthood, a holy nation, a peculiar people; that ye should shew forth the praises of him who hath called you out of darkness into his marvelous light* (1 Peter 2:9).

We often want to help God, but God never needed any help from anyone at any time, neither does He need our help in these last days. Even when we do not know what to say or do, He assures us that: *when they shall lead you, and deliver you up, take no thought beforehand what ye shall speak, neither do ye premeditate: but whatever shall be given you in that hour, that speak ye; for it is not ye that speak, but the Holy Ghost* (Mark 13:11). Our Creator knows more for His presence and wisdom will become our strength to help and save us. Our earthly achievements, knowledge or wisdom He does not need, but as a friend, He meets us saying: *whatsoever ye shall ask in my name, that will I do, that the Father may be glorified in the Son* (John 14:13) - 'whatsoever' includes physical, mental, spiritual, all wisdom and knowledge. 'Asking' means that we need talk to Him personally. When we talk to Him, He also gently guides and even teaches us what we should ask. Thus, when we ask Him for anything, our Friend shall give. We are commanded to ask and wait, for "they that wait upon the Lord ... renew their strength."

## Look What He Has Done

**ELISHA** - When Elijah was to be taken up to heaven, he told Elisha to stay behind. But Elisha had fixed his eyes on God for he knew that God had greater blessings for him too. Because he had waited upon God, he surely got what he had asked and also received the mantle of Elijah.

**SOLOMON** - had learned to trust God with all his heart. Therefore, God blessed him not only with an understanding heart, but also with riches, honor and long life. With such a submission, the Temple that he built was filled with the glory of God.

**MOSES** – When God called him from the burning bush, he fully grasped that there was nothing impossible with God. Thus, he followed God in all adversities. God greatly honored him by bringing the whole nation of Israel out of slavery. Following God faithfully caused even the Red Sea to part and honored the entire nation to walk on dry ground.

**JOHN** - the beloved disciple of the Lord, now an old man, but his loyalty to his Master was still his theme. Though exiled and left on the Island of Patmos, he discovered that he had an appointment with his Friend. Jesus met him and gave messages for all the churches. These warnings and admonitions are for the glory of His Church.

The Psalmist advises: *It is better to trust in the Lord than to put confidence in man* (Ps.118:8) for the mysteries of the Kingdom are still to be revealed to those who entirely trust Him regardless of their circumstances.

What He has done for others, He will do for us too.

## Unworthy Trust

There have been times when men of God have turned to others for help and found it disastrous. For example –

1. **Adam and Eve** in their innocence had full trust in each other and God. It was in that environment that Eve offered to Adam the fruit of the forbidden tree. Adam trusted Eve for he knew that beside God she was most trustworthy. He took her advice and paid no attention to what God had said. Thus, trusting the trustworthiness of Eve caused the fall of the entire human race.
2. **Judas Iscariot** trusted in wealth and worldly honor and lost everything.
3. **The Pharisees** knew the Scriptures for they were well entrenched in it. They had the knowledge, but it did not help them. The Messiah came and they heard Him speaking personally, but they rejected Him, though His coming was foretold. Their trust in their knowledge of the Scriptures and themselves blinded them. Knowing the Scriptures well, they used it for their own glory though God came in flesh to reach mankind. This led them to become stumbling block to many who wanted to know God intimately.
4. **Peter and some other disciples** went to Galilee to meet Jesus. Trusting their own expertise, they went fishing. Without Jesus, even the disciples learned they could not help themselves.

## Great Men Trust God

**MOSES** had acquired much knowledge in Egypt. But when he came to the other side of the mountain and met God, he received anointing which made him to lead the entire nation of Israel out of Egypt. Forgetting all who he was and his academic excellence, he completely put his hand in the hand of God and dared to do that no one ever did. He was simply persuaded that what God was doing only God could do which was greater than what man could ever conceive. His unwavering dependence on God favored the entire nation of Israel to go to freedom and then eventually to the promise land. God brought them out of Egypt and kept them under His cloud by day and His pillar of light by night. More so, God provided for all their physical needs and comforts. God also favored him to write the first five books of the Bible. Then when Jesus came, he presented himself at the Summit meeting that took place at the mount of Transfiguration – an honor that surpasses human mind.

**STEPHEN** though vehemently accused by fellow-believers, did not compromise his loyalty to God. Then as he prayed: *"Lord, lay not this sin to their charge"* (Acts 7:60), the heaven was charged with wonder as Jesus stood up for His faithful servant welcoming him in the mansions in glory. He died, but his faith and unbending love for Jesus still speaks to us, and he ever lives and witnesses the honor God wants to bestow upon all His faithful friends. Stephen did not count the cost because he knew that in God he could never fail. He has become an excellent example of submitting all to Jesus than all that is in the world. Now, it is for us to know that He is our real friend and that He, who wraps us in His love, demands all that we are.

**HISTORY** tells us that whenever Israel trusted in themselves and their neighbors' help, they were helpless to fight against their enemy, but every time they trusted God, they were victorious. Surely the Scripture says: *the Lord your God is he that goeth with you, to fight for you against your enemies, to save you* (Deuteronomy 20:4). God did fight all their battles, parted the sea for them, provided for all their needs in the wilderness journey, caused the river Jordan to stop flowing and thus enabled them to march into the promised land; kings were defeated, wall of Jericho came down, etc., etc. They triumphantly stepped into the land that flows with milk and honey. Now also is the time for the history to repeat. Therefore, be very diligent and wise for we also must walk with all the saints of history into the Promise Land. Doubts of all sorts lead us astray and mistrust speaks of only vanity.

**DAVID** had seen God's hand on him since his childhood. When he fought with Goliath, he found the earthly warrior armor too cumbersome. The only weapon of this small boy in the presence of two armies was his trust in God. When a single stone in his sling left, the Philistine army ran for their lives and could not prevail. When he was established in his kingdom and reminiscing that he was never bereaved of God's mercies and help, he wrote: *He brought me up also out of an horrible pit, out of the miry clay, and set my feet upon a rock, and established my goings* (Psalm 40:2). For his grateful heart and trust, he was called: *a man after his* (God's) *own heart* (1 Samuel 13:14). It seems he only knew the first commandment, which Jesus also quoted: *Thou shalt love the Lord thy God with all thy heart, and with all thy soul, and with all thy mind"* (Matthew 22:37-38). It was the secret of his greatness and will be ours too.

## Mighty and Ever Present

Our God, the Creator of the universe, is always with us. He has also endowed us with His Spirit. And Jesus said that He will: *teach you all things* (John 14:26). Jesus has promised great things for us, saying: *Ask and it shall be given you; seek ... knock, and it shall be opened unto you* (Matthew 7:7). He is sufficient to supply all our needs. Nothing is impossible with Him. For us His children, the Scriptures say: *I know the thoughts that I think toward you, saith the Lord, thoughts of peace, and not of evil* (Jeremiah 29:11). In His mercy and love, His sweet anointing awaits to refresh us. His plan for us is - to be born again and then to be filled with His Spirit. This is the real life for His children to walk in His light and anointing. He has equipped us for great things to be done with Him.

## Meet Jesus

Jesus anxiously wanted to meet with His disciples in His resurrection. Therefore, He said to Mary: *go tell my brethren that they go into Galilee, and there shall they see me* (Matthew 28:10). They were Galileans and He wanted to meet them in Galilee where they were living. So, He is anxious to meet us wherever we are.

They went to Galilee to the appointed place. Then they thought of going fishing because they had been fishermen. Even in their own expertise and environment they could not catch any fish till Jesus helped them. Sometime, we want to go to a place to do His work but get busy with other things in which we have an expertise. And then when we do not succeed, it is time to listen to Him who is calling us from the shore of our lives. We will surely find that His directions are so simple that when we do what He says, it will amaze us to receive His abundant blessings. The other disciples joined to help the catch. So likewise, the churches will rejoice to join together and will bring a huge multitude at the feet of Jesus. Then the Lord's Prayer will be answered: *That they all may be one* (John 17:21). Unity in the body of Christ, the Church, was in His heart, and this unity is possible only when we do precisely what He says and help each other before we get to the other side.

At this fishing ground, He asked His disciples, *Children, have ye any meat?* (John 21:5). The answer was 'no'. In our fishing ground, He likewise comes and wants to know how we are doing. He sees that many of us are busy evangelizing others, who are already saved. This is not fishing. We have forgotten that He has made us 'fishers of men' and says: *Go ye therefore into the highways, and as many as ye shall find, bid to the marriage* (Matthew 22:9). These are the people who are outside the fold. Their spirit is anxious to meet Jesus, as were the fish anxious to meet Jesus which were caught in the net, and were obedient to His call. Jesus wants to meet them. If they don't meet Jesus, should we not be afraid of Him who sees everything and has given us precise instructions? Jesus even said: *compel them to come in* (Luke 14:23). It seems the call is urgent.

After the disciples had brought the huge draw of fish to the shore, they understood the secret of listening to Him as they had suddenly become excellent fishermen, for He had told them: *Cast the net on the right side* (John 21:6). The right side is the right way that Jesus taught and has ordained for fishing men. It is written: *Jesus then cometh, and taketh bread, and giveth them, and fish likewise* (John 21:13). He had already prepared food for them and they all dined with Him. If we are fishers of men, He wants all of us to listen to Him and do what He says for Jesus invites us as well to dine with Him before we partake in the Lamb's supper in glory.

He then asked Peter thrice, 'do you love me'. After we have dined with Him, Jesus, in a small voice says to us in the same urgent fashion: *feed my lambs* (John 21:15). This was the call for humility and in sincere love. He knows that our minds get puffed up easily. Catching a large haul of fish at His bidding had humbled the disciples. Our catching of fish must keep us humble for in humility will be our joy of dining with Him. Wrong doctrines and heresies flourish in the absence of humility. Therefore: *Let this mind be in you, which was also in Christ Jesus* (Philippians 2:5) and feed His lambs. In the parable of the lost sheep, Jesus expressed His great love for the one that was lost, for He had said: *that likewise joy shall be in heaven over one sinner that repenteth, more than over ninety and nine just persons which need no repentance* (Luke 15:7). The lost ones are His lambs whom Jesus wants us to feed. It is our ambassadorial duty to obey Him fully and bring home the lost. We then surely shall see the showers of blessings. When we have done it all, we can expect to hear: *Well done, good and faithful servant … enter thou into the joy of thy lord* (Matthew 25:23).

Urgency is here. The need is great. People are perishing. Jesus has made us light in this world, and says: *Let your light so shine before men* (Matthew 5:16). If there is no light in us, or our lamps have not enough oil, it is written: *For thou wilt light my candle: the Lord my God will enlighten my darkness* (Psalm 18:28). Our humbly coming to Him and asking will expel the darkness out. Then the light will spring up for those who were/are sitting in darkness and shadow of death (Matthew 4:16). Jesus has anointed us to go and do His works. It will be regrettable if we are found working for Him but not obeying Him in this His very urgent commission. When we go out for those who are lost and bring them home, *there is joy in the presence of the angels of God over one sinner that repenteth* (Luke 15:10). This joy in heaven will cause blessings to be poured out in our ministries.

## We Are Commissioned

Jesus told His disciples: *Go ye into all the world, and **preach** the gospel to every creature* (Mark 16:15). *And they went forth, and preached every where, the Lord working with them, and confirming the word with signs following, Amen* (Mark 16:20). Jesus worked with them. And He works with those who do what He says. Working with Him is such a joy for: *No weapon that is formed against thee shall prosper* (Isaiah 54:17).

When preaching, we are reaching the ends of the earth, but we must do His will His way. Jesus said: *All power is given unto me in heaven and in earth. Go ye, therefore* (Matthew 28:18-19) for *lo, I am with you alway* (Matthew 28:20). He who sends us is with us, is the bright and morning star; King of kings and Lord of Lords and is the source of all wisdom. Doing His wishes with Him will astonish us, for we are His ambassadors. When we have done our mission on this earth and are called back home, it will be a joyous occasion of honor and glory in our Father's house. And while we are still here in the flesh, we can say: *surely goodness and mercy shall follow me all the days of my life* (Psalm 23:6) for "Thou preparest a table before me in the presence of my enemies" (Psalm 23:5). Our plea, therefore should be:

> *Lead me Lord, precious Jesus, Lead me to the higher ground.*
> *For when led by man, we have fallen, But with You, Jesus,*
> *we shall mount up as eagles.*

## Standard of God

The ever-changing world has made much inroad in the churches and made Church to conform to their standards. Therefore, we have mostly become the church of the world. In this maze when we have tried to raise our standard and see little result. But God's standard defined for her is for all ages. We cannot add or take away anything from it. Often in our business meetings, we try to see what we can do to make our churches more effective. Though our intentions are good, sometime we are caught in the intellectual maze of either pleasing man or God.

Our Lord has set the standard of humility for the church. With such a standard, the Bible says: *When the enemy shall come in like a flood; the Spirit of the Lord shall lift up a standard against him* (Isaiah 59:19).

For our ministries to be effective, Jesus said: "I am the way". If we follow His blueprint, we will find that He alone is sufficient to lead us. Sometime we are heavy laden with many problems in this world and in the churches. The voice from heaven still says: *this is my beloved Son; **hear him*** (Luke 9:35). When Jesus said: *For my yoke is easy and my burden is light.* He also said: *and I will give you rest* (Matthew 11:30,28). Isaiah had also said: *The yoke shall be destroyed because of the anointing* (Isaiah 10:27). If we believe that He is our burden bearer, the Church should be glorious.

## The Great Link

God has given us all wisdom for learning. It is good but much learning has often led many go astray from faith. A well learned person trusts more in the knowledge they have acquired. In Jesus' time also, the leaders, who were well learned and knew the Scriptures well, had let the sheep go astray. Jesus called some of them 'hypocrites' and wolves. Knowing well that man would always look to man, He was grieved. Therefore, Jesus had said: *Follow Me.* He also said: *Neither be ye called masters: for one is your Master, even Christ* (Matthew 23:9-10). Though Jesus had so many disciples who walked with Him and had learned at the feet of the Master of the Universe, He simply said: "Come unto me". Learned Apostle Paul has also said: *there is one God and one mediator between God and men, the man, Christ Jesus* (1 Timothy 2:5), the only way. This mediator wants all to come to Him. The tides of time have proved that His ways are far too excellent for they direct us on this earth and lead us all the way to eternal life. Can we hear Him saying: *I am come that you might have life* (John 10:10) and: *my peace I give unto you* (John 14:27)?

God made the heavens and the earth, the galaxies, and all things visible and invisible and He still looks after it all. Look, how He gives wisdom, life and strength to all His creation. He teaches even the newborn babies and gives them wisdom to know their new world they have stepped into. He has plans for their survival and for life more abundant too. For this abundant life, the Psalmist advises us: *that ye may tell it to the generation following* (Psalm 48:13). The life and light for the future generations also depend on us. It is our delight to tell the generations to come of this mediator, our Jesus, His love and His plan of salvation. This world must know its Creator for only in Him is our future glorious. We are all physical and spiritual, but the Bible tells us: *there is a spirit in man: and the inspiration of the Almighty giveth them understanding* (Job 32:8). Our spirit does receive understanding from God for all our physical needs. He also meets all our spiritual needs since we are also spiritual being.

## Getting Together

With a broken heart, Jesus said: *how often would I have gathered thy children together, even as a hen gathereth her chickens under her wings* (Matthew 23:37). Whenever we get together to pray and study the Word, we are under His wings. At such times, in that cozy atmosphere, we learn from the Master, as He has said: *where two or three are gathered together in my name, there am I in the midst of them* (Matthew 18:20). Thus, with our Friend and Father being among us, we forget our differences and He gently tells His children secrets of living abundant and victorious life. Then we understand the hidden treasures of the Kingdom.

But when we try to learn from others, human efforts come in and our minds make us believe more on our efforts. Apostle Paul, a scholar of his time, was such a person, but he confessed that all his previous knowledge was rubbish (Phil.3:8). Isaiah also says: *all our righteousness's are as filthy rags* (Isaiah 64:6). Therefore, for learning from Him, we ought to be seated at His feet. Then fountain of all knowledge breaks open for us and enriches us. For even Jesus' disciples said: *whom shall we go? thou hast the words of eternal life* (John 6:68). Thus, with such learning, people will say, How these people who are unlearned know so much?

## Heroes of God

For the last 2000 years, the world has witnessed great revivals. God's faithful servants dared to take the gospel to the lost. Some crossed over to their neighbors and others to the entire world and brought many to the kingdom of God. Some are famous, others, though silent, did valiantly. They made a difference in the world for God was much pleased to work with them. E.g., Martin Luther, John Bunyan, John Newton who caused revival in the U.K, Billy Graham, Sadhu Sunder Singh, Mel Tari, Paul Yonggi Cho, and unnumbered saints, driven by their love for Jesus, brought light to many in this dark world. It was their raptured love for the Lord that ignited the fire of God's love for mankind. They knew that what God had for them was far too glorious. When they heard Jesus saying to them: *Go ye into all the world* (Mark 16:15), they did not count the cost. Thus, churches started springing up wherever they went. People heard of the love of Jesus and calling upon His name many were transformed into the 'Children of light'. How precious were the words of Jesus in their ears who said: *I am the way, the truth, and the life* (John 14:6). For many, who sat under the shadow of death, saw the great Light. They were taught by God and did what the intellectuals had failed to do.

Now, instead of preaching the good news, the pulpits are sometime also used to justify and propagate denominational beliefs. Thus, the great commission took a new approach according to each denomination. It was for these sad moments that Jesus prayed earnestly, *that they all may be one* (John 17:22).

We have sold ourselves to new ideologies and forgotten the One who gave His life for us and holds the universe in His hands. How can we say that the Holy Spirit is our guide when we have chosen diversity and the worldly ways?

It is time to repent for we have lost much. Surely, Jesus, looking at the church today, says the same thing as He said to the Church of Laodiceans: *Because thou sayest, I am rich and increased with goods, and have need of nothing; and knowest not that thou art wretched, and miserable, and poor, and blind, and naked: I counsel thee to buy of me gold tried in the fire, that thou mayest be rich; and white raiment, that thou mayest be clothed, and that the shame of thy nakedness do not appear; and anoint thine eyes with eye salve, that thou mayest see* (Revelation 3:17-18). But be courageous and know that it is possible to recover it all if we would only let Jesus be Jesus and we be His dear sheep.

## What a Friend

Jesus is our redeemer, our nearest kinsman, and He also chose to call us His friends. See how He washed the feet of His disciples. Knowing who Jesus was, John the Baptist said: *He must increase, but I must decrease* (John 3:30). However, Jesus chose to decrease Himself so that we, His friends, might increase. And He has also conferred upon us a great honor to be His ambassadors here before we get to yonder glory. It was His great delight to say: *where I am, there ye may be also* (John 14:3). Studying from the Scriptures, we find that He has placed us at the divine level with Himself and the Father. In His rising from the dead, He has made us 'children of resurrection' and His emissaries and gave us all authority saying: *All power is given unto me in heaven and in earth. Go ye therefore* (Matthew 28:18-19). In bestowing His authority and blessings on us, He has fully equipped us to do His works. His love and concern for us reaches beyond all our abilities, theologies and understanding, for He gives us wisdom and power that this world is not able to fathom. Our Savior indeed is our friend and is our companion in all our ways.

## At Jesus' Feet

The woman of Samaria met Jesus at the well. There, talking to Him, she discovered that He is omniscient, the source of all wisdom, knowledge and salvation. It was in His simple way that He told her the true meaning of worship: "the hour cometh, and now is, when the true worshipers shall worship the Father in spirit and in truth" (John 4:23). Talking to Jesus and listening attentively to every word He said, she came to know that He was THE WAY of true worship. It was this worship that drew all in that village to come and know Jesus. They came and were overwhelmed as they listened to Him personally. Their hunger to receive more of Him was so great that they insisted Him to stay with them longer. For when she met Jesus, out of her belly flowed the rivers of living water. She drank from it and also the whole village people as they talked to Jesus.

Nicodemus had just gone to talk to Jesus and was the first to hear Him saying: "you must be born-again" to see and enter the kingdom of God. To his amazement, he and the whole world found that Jesus is the fountain of everlasting life. And that this life is for all generations who would come to Him. A conversation with Jesus thus opened the gates of heaven for all to know that God so loved the world.

Jesus Christ is all sufficient for meeting any physical, spiritual or mental needs. For, from Him, virtue and wisdom flow like a river. He quenches life's thirst of all who come to Him. This river never runs dry. Here, chains of sins are broken and healing virtues flow unceasingly. At Calvary, God in mercy meets us. His resurrection has enabled it for all times. He restores to humanity all that was lost since the event of the Garden of Eden.

We all need to come to Him and talk with Him for then we surely will find that the spiritual oasis is in sight for us to step in.

When we pray and our spirit is one with the Spirit of God, it is the time that we are sitting at the very feet of our Master. Isaiah says: *and I will make the place of my feet glorious* (Isaiah 60:13). Mary found the joy of worshipping when she found a resting place at His feet. Such are the moments when secrets of His love are revealed, relationships are restored and His glory and blessings become ours. And like dew, heaven comes down and empowers us to declare His majesty and glory.

## Rejoicing in Cosmic Sphere

In the cosmic sphere, the stars and galaxies obey God to keep their path. They never cease to witness their obedience to their Creator by shining so brightly. The earth also obeys the order designed by its Creator to revolve in the cosmic sphere in her majestic fashion. Beside this, she, without fail, provides food for all its dwellers and meets all their needs. God created the entire universe with a perfect design. He also has plans for each one of us living in this His world which is far too excellent. Since we too are His creation, He expects the same loyalty from us to do His will. Our lives therefore must show forth His glory naturally. Also, our lives should be as is evident from the faithfulness of our earth and the cosmic worlds. It seems the whole universe is calling us to join in that fathomless excellent joy.

The Bible tells us that the heaven and the earth made music to His glory. This was and is their continued worship. But we have been influenced by many cultures and become their slaves. We have forgotten that we are God's children and ambassadors. If we would not do His will, His eternal plans will be carried out by others who will make us wander like the five foolish virgins. Though we think that we are doing His works, and are ready to enter into His glory, we might miss out entering into His gates. And if we are found outside and calling Him, will we then justify ourselves on the judgment day when an account is required of us all and still hear the words: *I do not know you?* We must look at the universe, in the Scriptures, and then at our own heart. The Bible admonishes us to *Keep thy heart with all diligence; for out of it are the issues of life* (Proverbs 4:23), for out of our hearts must flow rivers of living water (John 7:38). Surely, the Scriptures encourage us to do the works of our Father and our Friend.

## Short Sighted

A carnally minded person may think he is weak. But the fact is that we have the capability of reaching the heaven and touch eternity. Therefore, apostle Paul pleads: *be not conformed to this world, but be ye transformed by the renewing of your mind, that ye may prove what is that good, and acceptable, and perfect, will of God* (Romans 12:2). Without the perfect will of God in our lives, we have become short sighted. We do not realize that our life is like a leaf that may fall at any stroke of time. But in Christ Jesus, our strength can be renewed as of an eagle and in His might are able to do unheard things. When we cooperate with our Friend, He will be working with us.

## Lot's Loss

Lot was brought up by Abraham and had certainly heard many things from him about God's leadings before he dwelt in Sodom with his family. Abraham was, therefore, sure that because of Lot, there would be a few righteous persons in Sodom and Gomorrah. The time came and God, having heard the cry of those cities, came to visit them. Abraham, knowing that if things were not good there, God's judgment would be severe. So he pleaded with God for fifty righteous men thinking that Lot and his family must have led some to fear and trust God. Eventually, he came down to plead even for ten. Lot's family had not led even that many to trust God. His neglect of not telling them of the fear of God resulted in these cities, where he was living, being destroyed, and even his own wife becoming a pillar of salt. Life's sole purpose is not to live here and tell others of our plans but to tell God's saving power. Jesus' mission was that none should perish. It was important then and is important now. When Jesus first called His disciples, He said: "Follow me, and I will make you fishers of men" (Matthew 4:19). He has passed on this mission to all who believe in Him. His desire to save others was so emphatic that He even said: *Go out into the highways and hedges, and* **compel them** *to come in* (Luke 14:23). For this very reason, He willingly gave His life on the cross so that we may not perish. His life and resurrection proved that it was His mission. Therefore, He gave us the great commission to go, preach and teach. The word 'teach' is often misunderstood. It implies to teach obedience to the Word of God and to fear God. God alone is our teacher and Master and has given us power and authority in heaven and on earth to do the works that He did. With such a divine leading and power, how can we think of earthly wisdom and ways to do His work? Ours is the heavenly calling and, as His followers, we should trust Him and be willing to do His will in this world and in our lives and bring those who are lost to the Kingdom of God. Trusting only half the way is disobedience and is very dangerous.

Like Lot's wife, we may not make to safety. Or like the five foolish virgins, we may find the door closed on us.

## Let Us Go

In His discourse on the Mount of Olives, Jesus told His disciples: *Arise, let us go hence* (John.14.31b). They went with Him to Calvary, and Calvary led them to resurrection. It was then that they came to know the power of resurrection and that height of glory was not a mystery any more. Today, He calls us the same way. Look, He took away all our sins and burdens at Calvary and has made us 'children of resurrection'. Since then, His faithful followers went filled with His Spirit to do what He Himself was doing. He commissioned all those that follow Him, to do the same. Thus, the Church grew alarmingly because they were faithful, and did not look at herself or the world, but to God. Since He calls us, let us sincerely say to Him: 'Lord, I come. Let us go together. We want to go and work along with you'. Because, with God: *the weapons of our warfare are not carnal, but mighty through God to the pulling down of strong holds* (2 Corinthians 10:4).

## Triumphs of Obedience

King David said about his son, Solomon: *Solomon my son is young and tender, and the house that is to be builded for the Lord must be exceeding magnifical, of fame and of glory throughout all countries* (1 Chronicles 22:5). **The CHURCH is the glory of God.** It must excel in magnificence and reveal the exceeding great glory of God. But, she has received only a drizzle of His blessings just because of the name of Jesus. He wants to shower her and drench her in His abundant blessings. But we have depended on Him only half way. For such, Jesus said with a broken heart: "verily I say unto you, ye shall not see me, until the time come when ye shall say: Blessed is he that cometh in the name of the Lord" (Luke 13:35). Obedience is Christianity.

O CHURCH, RISE AND SHINE. Put off the garments of pride and self. Isaiah has joyously declared: "for thy light is come, and the glory of the Lord is risen on thee" (Isaiah 60.1). And to us, who are His light in this world, Jesus says: *Let your light ... shine* (Matthew 5:16). The time to shine again is here, is now and will be our glory. Amen.

# I Will Build

Jesus had asked his disciples: *...whom say ye that I am?* Peter's reply was: *Thou art the Christ, the Son of the living God.* Jesus then said: *...and upon this rock I will build my church; and the gates of hell shall not prevail against it* (Matthew 16:15,16,18). Here Jesus declared, ***I will build my church.*** Jesus is the architect and builder of His Church. No other can build it. Denominations, all earthly efforts and theological knowledge cannot build it. Organizations, who have tried to build it by their own efforts, have not heeded this statement seriously. The Church that Christ builds is able to overcome the enemy. Yes, such a Church has the power even to pull down the gates of hell.

Jesus, being the author and architect of this Church, went Himself down to hell and the gates of hell could not prevail against Him. *And the graves were opened; and many bodies of the saints which slept arose, And came out of the graves after his resurrection, and went into the holy city, and appeared unto many* (Matthew 27:52-53). The gates of hell could not prevail against Christ and they also will not prevail against His Church. Therefore, let Christ build us for without His help our efforts are futile.

We all have built churches carefully and want to fill these with people which also reflect our effort to make these very attractive. But the Church Jesus had in mind is far more glorious because it reflects God's glory. Our purpose should be that it be filled with the glory of God. If it is otherwise, it will reflect our efforts only. Therefore, let the Spirit of God have His sway and it will surprise us what God does for us.

Of the first century Church, the Bible reports: ***the Lord added*** to *the church daily such as should be saved* (Acts 2:47). The One who is the builder is also the One who adds to its numbers. Almost every church and denomination are frantic to increase its membership. For this purpose, records are kept of attendees, programs are devised, new and magnificent buildings are erected, and sanctuaries are made attractive and comfortable to draw people in.

There are great denominations with large memberships. Some keep growing. This has been the result of efforts over hundreds of years. However, Church growth recorded in the book of Acts was phenomenal. She was a dynamic force in the world when Christ was building her. When human efforts took charge, we slowly landed in the Dark Ages. Two thousand years of effort has also brought many heresies. Instead of harmony in the churches, feuds play a major role.

Families are split. For example, in a so-called Christian marriage, if one person is a member of a particular denomination which is different from the partner's, that family focuses mostly on the differences. Many Christian homes have been split because of these differences. Their differences affect their children, who, seeing contention among their parents on spiritual matters, think of Christianity as something to refrain from. For them, it seems Christianity only creates discord rather than harmony. The Gospel of love to these children becomes confusion. Because of disunity between the parents, children receive no spiritual guidance and become rebellious.

Jesus certainly did not come to build such churches. Their antagonism for each other is well known by their denominational banners. Someone might say that it is not fair to make such statements about churches that are already there, and denominations which have done so much for the glory of God.

The first century Church was dynamic, for daily many people were added to her. The popularity of such a vibrant Church had become widely known. It attracted the attention of many kings who embraced Christianity. Some became Christians because they were convicted of her truths. Others joined for political reasons. They had noticed that the Church was a dynamic force of the future and were shrewd in their manipulation of Christianity to maintain their own political control. They knew that she was also socially accepted by almost everyone. Thus, they embraced Christianity for political gain also. And among these, there were many who did not want to forsake their old customs, traditions and celebrations of festivities. Hence, instead of renouncing these, they put the old wine into new bottles. Because they were kings and political leaders, nobody could oppose them. Alas! The people were plunged into pseudo-Christianity. Hence many heathen practices were made part of their new Christian faith as the old life customs and practices also became customs and practices in so called Christendom. Each ruler introduced different customs.

Hence various styles of worship and beliefs were introduced giving birth to denominations. This adulterated Christianity choked real spiritual values and the spread of Christianity was halted. In such times of darkness, other religions leaped forward. The true light of the Gospel became dim in organized churches which pledged allegiance to their sovereign's wishes and the churches were willing to give their allegiance also to politicians and earthly authorities.

In the absence of help from the Holy Spirit, men became ritualistic and the churches had no blessing from above. Truly *the body without the spirit is dead* (James 2:26).

## Faith Works

As the Dark Ages dawned, faith was slowly becoming a scarce commodity being choked by new edicts. Religious leaders submitted to political pressures hoping to receive honor and respect and the freedom to live peacefully.

To have a complete sway over their affairs, these leaders made it difficult for common people to have access to the Word of God. They made themselves the sole custodians of the Scriptures. While they themselves remained in darkness, they let traditions, pomp and ceremony of religiosity flourish to retain their prestigious positions. They also found it politically expedient to add to these traditions. Idol worship also stepped in which was abhorred in the Old Testament and never encouraged in the early Church. It became the norm in many churches. Churches sanctified these practices and more heresies began breeding.

## Learning from Samson

The life of Samson in the Old Testament gives us encouragement because he faced somewhat similar circumstances. Samson was appointed by God to: *be a Nazarite unto God from the womb: and he shall begin to deliver Israel out of the hand of the Philistines* (Judges 13:5). His strength was in his hair which was not to be shorn. However, through his wife Delilah, his enemies cut off his hair and his strength departed. God likewise has chosen us to be His servants. Like Samson, we also have allowed our strength in the Lord to be shaved off for worthless worldly wisdom, honors and prestige. This has caused blindness for centuries and has left many of us still groping in the Dark Ages. It seems that our very eyes have been taken away by our religious peers who have cooperated with political and religious authorities to rule over us for centuries. These chains are still upon us.

While Samson was a prisoner of the Philistines, his hair had begun to grow. By the time he cried to the Lord requesting another opportunity, his hair had grown considerably. God wants to give us another opportunity. Many revivals have let our hair (our faith) grow in the sight of the Lord. Now our faith must rise up in us as we cry to God to restore unto us His strength—*they that wait upon the Lord shall renew their strength* (Isaiah 40:31). In our own strength, we have been blind. Let it now not be our strength, but His.

*And Samson called unto the Lord, and said, O Lord God, remember me, I pray thee, and strengthen me, I pray thee, only this once, O God, that I may be at once avenged of the Philistines for my two eyes* (Judges 16:28). Samson prayed to God for strength to avenge his two eyes. We too should pray to God to strengthen us once again.

The enemy has taken our eyes away so we cannot see the things God has for us. *And Samson said, Let me die with the Philistines. And he bowed himself with all his might; and the house fell upon the lords, and upon all the people that were therein. So the dead which he slew at his death were more than they which he slew in his life* (Judges 16:30).

His prayer was, *'let me die.'* When he prayed this, he died to himself. Then the strength of the Lord came upon him as he took revenge on his enemies before his death. Like Samson, we too must die to ourselves. I encourage anyone who is God's chosen to be like Samson. As Samson bowed himself with all his might, he was able to reduce a massive structure to rubble. That structure was gone and all people in it, but the children of Israel were delivered. God's people who depend on God must dare to do as Samson did. We too must be able to pull down the strongholds of our enemy by strength that comes from calling upon the Name of the Lord.

The Bible says: *love him with all the heart ... and with all the strength (Mark 12:33)*. Because when we love Him, His strength becomes ours. The source of this strength is Christ's mighty resurrection. When Samson prayed "let me die," he became resurrected as the strength of the Lord came upon him. The same power will come to us when we die to ourselves and rise up renewed in His might. Before the time closes on us, let us exchange our strength with His so that we may bring end-time victories to our Lord. His victories will be ours too and we shall gladly enter into His joy.

# A Limping Church

The first century Church was vibrant and victorious, and her glory had spread to all the then known world. Though it went through horrifying times of persecution, torture and imprisonment, nothing could deter her advancement because she leaned entirely on the Lord Jesus and the Holy Spirit was their guide.

Christianity took its leap into the nations as many peoples found the One who said: *I am the way, the truth, and the life* (John 14:6) and many kings also became Christian. Hence Christianity became the national religion of those countries. But sadly, in this new walk of life, many heathen practices found their way in also. There in the comfort of these political canopies her fervour was lost. She started groping in darkness and weeds of worldly riches and wealth choked her. Gradually true Christianity was being replaced by ordinances of the newly established churches which strove for power and earthly treasures. New ideologies that had crept in resulted in more denominations springing up with each promoting their own vision for the Church.

**Efforts of Recovery**

Deep in our heart we know there is much more life for the Church than what we see or can even dream of. For as the deer longs for the water, the Church found the living water as the revivals brought life to the lost.

Often in prayer I have asked the Lord why churches today are so weak and divided. The Holy Spirit sadly pointed out: 'The churches are limping." He also pointed out that they are limping because they are not fulfilling the Great Commission. The authority and power that Christ has given to her are not operational in her.

## Threefold Ministry

*And Jesus went about all Galilee, teaching in their synagogues, and preaching the gospel of the kingdom, and healing all manner of sickness and all manner of disease among the people* (Matthew 4:23).

We observe here that Jesus had a threefold ministry: (1) He went; (2) teaching and preaching gospel of the kingdom; (3) and healing all manner of sickness and all manner of disease. If it is said about Moses, *Moses was faithful in all his house* (Hebrews 3:2), how much more do we have to be faithful to the three-fold ministry Jesus has committed to the Church in the Great Commission: to go, to preach and to heal in Jesus name. Who also said that *they will cast out demons … they will lay hands on the sick, and they will recover* (Mark 16:17-18). This threefold ministry has never ended. For when Jesus on the cross cried and said: It is finished, His work was finished, but when He gave this three-fold Great Commission to the disciples, our work started. The churches have gone, preached the gospel, but healing part is left out for debating mostly. Hence, we have not obeyed the Great Commission completely. Though the Bible says that those who were sick received healing and many saints who were dead came back to life on that glorious resurrection morning, and so it happened in the early Church. The book of Acts also confirms that God was working miracles through believing Christians for: *the Lord working with them, and confirming the word with signs following. Amen* (Mark 16:20). For Jesus had said: *the works that I do shall ye do also* (John 14:12).

Today, things are different. It is sad that though we go and preach, but attach little importance to physical healing which is significant part of His commission. The Great Commission says -

*Go:* Jesus said: *go into all the world.* We are already in the world. The mission field is all around us and there is plenty of fish where we are. The work must start wherever He has placed us, whether in the environment we are or in a foreign land for Jesus is with us always and everywhere.

*Teaching and Preaching:* The Great Commission demands and commanded that we preach the Gospel to every creature: *Teaching them* *to observe **all things** whatsoever I have commanded you"* (Matthew 28:20). 'All things' definitely means that no exclusion is permitted irrespective of ideologies. In its unadulterated form, the Gospel has the anointing from above, is definitely effective and bears much fruit for the kingdom of God. We have believers in almost every part of the world. Since this Commission is given to all believers everywhere, if believers everywhere will undertake this eternal task, this world will glow with the light so gloriously.

***Healing:*** The importance of healing caused Jesus to go everywhere, preaching the Gospel, and all the four gospels speak loudly that He was *healing all manner of sickness and all manner of disease among the people.* So, He commands us to do - to *lay hands on the sick, and they shall recover* (Mark 16:18). As the disciples obeyed and did what the Lord had told them, this good news was reported: ... *the Lord working with them, and confirming the word with signs following* (Mark 16:20). When Jesus said: *I am with you alway, even unto the end of the world* (Matthew 28:20), no fear should stop us for we are in the company of Jesus. It is for us to obey, and Jesus, the Healer, will do what He did when He was on this earth.

*Jesus Christ the same yesterday, and to day and for ever* (Hebrews 13:8). All that He did during His ministry on this earth and in the early Church, was the demonstration for us. Now it is for us to show forth His greatness by doing as instructed by Him. For this reason, Jesus said, *Let your light so shine before men, that they may see your good works, and glorify your Father which is in heaven* (Matthew 5:16).

Isaiah accepted the challenge when he was asked: *Whom shall I send, and who will go for us.* He replied: *Here am I; send me* (Isaiah 6:8). Isaiah could say this because he had seen the glory of God. We in the churches need to meet God, see His glory and then go and do the works that He wants us to do. Remember, Jesus has emphatically said: *He that believeth on me, **the works that I do** shall he do also; and greater works than these shall he do; because I go unto my Father. And whatsoever ye shall ask in my name, that will I do, that the Father may be glorified in the Son. If ye shall ask any thing in my name, **I will do it*** (John 14:12-14). It is joy full of glory to do His works because we will find Jesus working with us every step of the way.

Satan has always tried to negate God's commands. He cunningly deals with the Great Commission too. He tells us, "You must go and preach the gospel to the entire world. Go far from your home because the world over there is in darkness." In short, he wants us to believe that the world is yonder. To such workers who are in the mission fields and work in God's vineyard, the devil says, 'Well! Haven't you done enough already? You are not God. You cannot heal.' But Jesus simply said: *lay hands on the sick, and they shall recover* (Mark 16:18). The Lord worked with the early Church because they obeyed Him: *the Lord working with them* (Mark 16:20). He worked with them and wants to work with us too. The result speaks for itself: *signs following them.* Healing comes from the One who is THE HEALER. Even Moses writes that God says: *for I am the Lord that healeth thee* (Exodus 15:26). We are bound with Jesus in love on the cross and nothing shall be impossible.

# Rebuild the Temple

The temple in Jerusalem was destroyed by King Nebuchadnezzar, and the children of Israel were taken captive to Babylon. Destruction and captivity came because the people of Judah continued to live in spite of warnings from God about their disobedience.

Years later, the work of rebuilding the temple of God in Jerusalem was undertaken by Governor Zerubbabel of Judea, High Priest Joshua and those who had returned from their captivity. But on their return to Jerusalem, the people were busy building their own houses and there was no blessing - *Ye have sown much, and bring in little; ye eat, but ye have not enough; ye drink but ye are not filled with drink; ye clothe you, but there is none warm; and he who earneth wages earneth wages to put into a bag with holes* (Haggai 1:6).

*Because of mine house that is waste* and *ye run every man unto his own house. Therefore the heaven over you is stayed from dew, and the earth is stayed her fruit. And I called for a drought upon the land, and upon the mountains, and upon the corn, and upon the new wine and upon the oil, and upon that which the ground bringeth forth, and upon men, and upon cattle, and upon all the labour of the hands* (Haggai 1:9-11).

Such seems to be the condition of many Christians and church organizations. Though many have returned from the exile of sin, they occupy themselves in building their own personal lives or denominations. They think they are doing fine, but the dew and fruit from the ground is stayed from them. Also because of drought, mankind is crying out for spiritual food. There is also not much blessing upon our efforts. God's house is in ruins because of the preoccupation of Christians with their own lives which keeps them busy, while the land and people lie desolate.

It is time to seek the Lord to reside in His glory among us. In Jerusalem, the walls of the city were down and danger was lurking upon her day and night. In churches, our self-centeredness and lukewarm heart towards God should have no place for we are the temple of God and house of blessing for the nations.

*Then Zerubbabel the son of Shealtiel, and Joshua the son of Josedech, the high priest, with all the remnant of the people, obeyed the voice of the Lord their God, and the words of Haggai the prophet, as the Lord their God had sent him, and the people did fear before the Lord. Then spake Haggai, the Lord's messenger in the Lord's message unto the people, saying, I am with you, saith the Lord* (Haggai 1:12-13).

It is exciting to know that when we obey the Lord and fear Him, His blessings will flow like a river. When the children of Israel obeyed God, the blessings overflowed as the Temple was restored completely. On another occasion, the wall of Jerusalem was similarly repaired in just fifty-two days (Nehemiah 6:15) and the enemy was shut out of the city. Blessings of God will definitely come if the spiritual house within each one of us is repaired. It is the working of the Holy Spirit with us that will bring glory to us in His name and we will be able to execute God's commission. It will be accomplished in such a short time that it will surprise everyone.

Zechariah had prophesied about building the temple of God in Jerusalem: *Moreover, the word of the Lord came unto me, saying, The hands of Zerubbabel have laid the foundation of this house; his hands shall also finish it; and thou shalt know that the Lord of hosts hath sent me unto you* (Zechariah 4:8-9). God has indeed sent Jesus unto us who has laid the foundation of the Church and it is only He who shall also finish it. *For other foundation can no man lay than that is laid, which is Christ Jesus* (1 Corinthians 3:11). Since Jesus has laid the foundations of His Church, let us allow Him to finish it too. For it is going to be His magnificent structure and must show forth His glory. No organization can help God to establish it, no educational faculty is capable of finishing it, no church organization can boast of their capabilities. It is Jesus only who shall finish it.

Sometimes when we build a church, we give it the name of the denomination or ministry. It indirectly edifies us. If Christ is governor under whom it is to be built, it surely should reflect God's glory. When Zerubbabel rebuilt the temple, he did not call it Zerubbabel's temple of God. Later, when the same temple was repaired by Herod, it was called Herod's temple. We follow Herod's example. Though we might add the word 'church' to it, it surely propagates human pride.

Nobody can take credit for building God's temple. Denominations through education and wealth have tried to make it so attractive. However, all our efforts have not helped us against the continual onslaught of the enemy. Our lives, which are the temple of God, are still in ruins. Jesus said: *And I will pray the Father, and he shall give you another Comforter, that he may abide with you for ever* (John 14:16). Only the Holy Spirit in us can build us for the glory of God. When He builds us, *we all, with open face beholding as in a glass the glory of the Lord, are changed into the same image from glory to glory, even as by the Spirit of the Lord* (2 Corinthians 3:18).

In the Book of Revelation, the One who said: *I am Alpha and Omega, the first and the last* (Revelation 1:11), also addressed the seven churches. In His message to the church in Laodicea, He said: *Because thou sayest, I am rich, and increased with goods, and have need of nothing; and knowest not that thou art wretched, and miserable, and poor, and blind, and naked.* (Revelation 3:17). Man looks at the external riches, but the Lord looks at the heart. Riches in Christ are not comparable to the riches of the world. The riches of the world are temporary, riches in Christ are eternal.

The prince of this world has indeed blinded the eyes of many of us by worldly wealth, honour and the flesh. God, however, still says: *I counsel thee to buy gold tried in the fire, that thou mayest be rich; and white raiment, that thou mayest be clothed … and anoint thine eyes with eye salve, that thou mayest see. As many as I love, I rebuke and chasten; be zealous therefore, and repent. Behold, I stand at the door and knock; if any man hear my voice, and open the door, I will come in to him, and will sup with him, and he with me* (Revelation 3:18-20).

This indeed is good news that the door is still open. The invitation is extended, the table is made ready and God wants us to come and eat with Him. *To him that overcometh will I grant to sit with me in my throne, even as I also overcame, and am set down with my Father in his throne* (Revelation 3:21), repenting of all that they have done for their own glory. Indeed, coming to Him is all gain and obeying Christ is glorious.

We know that our lives, though they may look very glamorous, are in ruins. On the other hand, Jesus says: *Behold, I stand at the door* (Revelation 3:20). He has the riches, clothes of His righteousness and ointment for our blindness with Him. We can only be built a spiritual house by the Spirit of God. Also, God wills that our house be built for His glory only, for He is our glory. He can change us and fill our lives with His Spirit. If we would humbly come before God and repent of our pride, we will comfortably be able to bear the cross that Jesus wants us to carry. Once we have humbled ourselves before Him and are willing to bear our cross, we have started building the broken temple of our lives. The lamp in our life will then shine brightly by Jesus, the Light of the world. Jesus, lights it and we can say: *Thy word is a lamp unto my feet, and a light unto my path* (Psalm 119:105). Praise God, He wants to rebuild us.

The hymn writer has states it so well:

> *Just as I am without one plea,*
> *But that Thy blood was shed for me,*
> *And that Thou bidd'st me come to Thee,*
> *O Lamb of God, I come! I come!*

> *Just as I am, poor, wretched, blind;*
> *Sight, riches, healing of the mind,*
> *Yea all I need, in Thee I find,*
> *O Lamb of God, I come! I come!*
>          *- Charlotte Elliott, 1789-1871.*

# My House is in Ruins

Prophet Haggai was contemporary of Zechariah at the time Zerubbabel was the governor of Judea. The exiles had returned to Jerusalem from Babylon. They had been in captivity because they had forgotten God. Their return had now given them the freedom to worship God who had delivered them from their captivity. But they were busy building their paneled houses while the temple of God still lay in ruins.

God told the people of Israel through prophet Haggai: *Go up to the mountain, and bring wood, and build the house; and I will take pleasure in it, and I will be glorified, saith the Lord* (Haggai 1:8).

About the temple of God, the New Testament states: *Know ye not that ye are the temple of God, and that the Spirit of God dwelleth in you?* (1 Corinthians 3:16). Paul also states: *If any man defile the temple of God, him shall God destroy; for the temple of God is holy, which temple ye are* (1 Corinthians 3:17)? His question, *'which temple you are'* is still penned by the Holy Spirit for us to respond.

If any man defile the temple of God, him, Apostle Paul says, shall God destroy. To do His will is what God wants. It applies to all individuals as well as the churches. The fabric of our churches is so fragile as there is no unity among them. Therefore, God says to them also: *Go up to the mountain, and bring wood, and build the house.*

God also told the prophet Haggai to tell the people: ... *Consider your ways. Ye have sown much, and bring in little; ye eat, but ye have not enough; ye drink, but ye are not filled with drink; ye clothe you, but there is none warm; and he that earneth wages earneth wages to put it in a bag with holes* (Haggai 1:5-6). Looking at their pathetic lives, God commanded these former exiles to go up to the mountain and bring wood. When they obeyed and started to do it, the temple of God was once again the glory of the nations.

This also happened in the New Testament. Wood was brought which formed a cross on a hill called Calvary. The Church is built on the foundation on which cross Jesus died for all mankind. When we join ourselves to that cross, we are doing well. However, the words of prophet Haggai are still in the present tense: *Go up to the mountain, and bring wood.* We all need to go to the mountain, in faith, where Jesus died. Then looking and talking to Him, as did the other thief on the cross, we die to our old self but rise up to build the temple. Then we know that He is with us. Then with the psalmist we will say: *I will lift up mine eyes unto the hills, from whence cometh my help* (Psalm 121:1). Whenever we go to the mountains, naturally we look at their peaks. These peaks all point us to heaven as though they are saying, don't look at us but look to the One who has made us and is in heaven. Yes, He is the only One from where our help will come.

The wooden cross was carried to Calvary half the way by Jesus and half of the way by a man. In prophet Haggai's saying: *go up to the mountain, and bring wood,* a much bigger mystery was to be revealed in time. Now it was at Calvary where the work of building the temple of God was implemented. It means that we too, like the exiles who had returned from captivity, have to go to that mountain, carry the wood and build God's house. When they obeyed God, the gigantic task of rebuilding the temple was accomplished in no time and God was glorified.

The building of the wall of Jerusalem also took place in the midst of opposition from the enemies in the form of mockery and conspiracy. Beside all efforts of the enemy to disrupt its progress, the work was completed in just fifty-two days with God's blessing. When we obey God, His help is certain and is great indeed.

The phrase, *'and bring wood'* is also in the present tense and is intended for us. Action is required on our part that we have to pick up wood and build God's temple. Like the man who picked up cross for Jesus, we have to carry it. For Jesus said: *Whosoever will come after me, let him deny himself, and take up his cross, and follow me* (Mark 8:34).

Unless we take up our cross, we will not do well for the house of God is in ruins.

But when we pick up our cross, the house of God is already in the process of building. The completion of our paneled houses on this earth is not mentioned anywhere, but God's house once again becomes the glory of all the nations. It was and is for the glory of God to dwell in it and for us to enter into His glory. The words of Jesus: *My house shall be called the house of prayer; but ye have made it a den of thieves* (Matthew 21:13), should wake us up.

If we are His temple, is this temple a house of prayer? Are our churches, in Christ's words, a house of prayer or are we the dens of thieves, now dwelling amidst the riches of this world?

Many cities are known for their cathedrals and magnificent architectural edifices. They are carefully designed to show the excellence of time and organization. These fantastic structures fill us with awe at man's capability and craftsmanship. Inside these artifices are paintings and sometime statues of man's concept of God. Practices in the world's religions are not any different. Buddhists use the prayer wheel. Others pray a certain number of times a day. Some even afflict their bodies thinking that God will be appeased by such acts. There are others who engage in some strict discipline, like monastic exercises.

These disciplines make them think they are pleasing their deity. These are human exercises which make them think that, by such doings, their god will be pleased by their acts. Such exercises are also prevalent in many churches where pleasing God through their deeds is the norm. We also have taken pride in establishing denominations and there are buildings that add to their name. Then there are missionary efforts to make their name known everywhere. If it is all done for the glory of God, why can we not tolerate other brothers and sisters in Christ? Instead of loving each other, why we sometime cannot tolerate others?

Where is our love for one another? The One who has commanded us to *Go into all the world* has also told us to *love one another.* How can we be jealous for God and hate each other and yet say we are pleasing God? While the Scriptures say: *ye are the temple of God,* we say, 'look at our efforts, our denomination, our monumental buildings.' When the disciples had showed Him the temple building, Jesus said to them: *See ye not all these things? verily I say unto you, There shall not be left here one stone upon another, that shall not be thrown down* (Matthew 24:2).

Saying these things about the end times, Jesus said, it shall also be a time, when *knowledge shall be increased* (Daniel 12:4). While there is no lack of knowledge in our many churches, love for each other has diminished considerably. God's way and knowledge are much higher than what we have or can ever imagine. Every time the nation of Israel ignored God and did not heed the warnings of the prophets, calamities came upon them. When Jesus used such strong words about the temple in Jerusalem, He was also inferring to the spiritual decline of the nation. He surely is saying the same today to the people who call themselves by His name. When He looks at the condition of our hearts, where His glory should dwell, He sees ruins because of our spiritual lethargy. God's heart was and is always much grieved when our hearts became spiritually cool.

*Because of mine house that is waste, and ye run every man unto his own house. Therefore the heaven over you is stayed from dew, and the earth is stayed from her fruit* (Haggai 1:9-10). God sees us also that we all run to our house, denomination or ministry. Whereas we should be going to God directly, we have our small places which are the pride of each one of us. When we are concerned about ourselves, our hearts where God should reside, remain desolate. No doubt, God's untold blessings are not with us because God is not in the temple and the earth has stayed her fruit from us.

But prophet Haggai has not left us in darkness. God, who knew that many of us would carry the wood, said: *The glory of this latter house shall be greater than of the former, saith the Lord of hosts: and in this place will I give peace* (Haggai 2:9). If we would build our churches and lives according to God's plans, the Church on earth would have no equal. We will erect the foundations of God's temple in us and in our communities and complete His work.

## The Latter Temple

The Holy Spirit in us is to bless and empower us to be faithful to do all He has commanded us; *Not by might, nor by power, but by my spirit, saith the lord of hosts* (Zechariah 4:6). The gentle Holy Spirit enables us to bear our cross too. He will make the latter temple of our beings glorious. These words were not given for the nation of Israel only but are written so that all nations through all generations might know how their latter spiritual temple can be greater than the former too.

Every believer and every church can hope that their future can be blessed beyond all expectation. So far, most churches and denominations have been clothed in the robes of pride and achievements. Though they profess God, their strife is not over. What God said through Haggai, so he says to all: *Go to the mountain, and bring wood.* If all individuals, denominations and ministries would go to the holy mountain, take wood for themselves, bear their cross as Simon bore Christ's, the temple of God will be filled with His glory. For Jesus has said: *If any man will come after me, let him deny himself, and take up his cross, and follow me* (Matthew 16:24).

Most of our activities are wrapped up in rituals. Our educational superiority and worldly dignity have given us great prestige. Our administrative abilities, missionary efforts, social services, and the list goes on have been our song. Alas! God's glory has been replaced by worldly glory.

The latter house has got to be built on humility and love, and in obedience guided by the Holy Spirit. It will show the majesty, glory and power of our Lord as believers join hands in the love of God. Under such a holy canopy of love, God's glory will fill this house and we shall have the anointing of joy. We will also know the wonders of serving God. Then His blessings on every phase of our activity will be upon us when we join hands with each other and with Him in carrying out the Great Commission. The signs will follow. We will then be able to witness to the world which has been alienated from the Kingdom of God by our human efforts.

True knowledge of eternal life comes only from Christ Jesus and it comes when we meet Him. Saul heard the words of Jesus when *suddenly there shined round about him a light from heaven: And he fell to the earth, and heard a voice saying unto him, Saul, Saul, why persecutest thou me?* (Acts 9:3-4). That light is still shining around us and Jesus is still saying to us, 'why persecutest thou me.'

Unless we meet Jesus we cannot work for Him. A graduate or a postgraduate degree or any other earthly commission is not the prerequisite for the Master's service. This is a spiritual ministry. These degrees give comfort and prestige, but meeting Christ personally gives the power from above. Spiritual matters can only be discerned spiritually. Therefore, spiritual gifts are necessary because the Holy Spirit alone teaches us in all our service to the Master and in spiritual matters. All things written in the Bible are for our admonition and cannot be replaced by any human faculty or any spiritual power. Paul, therefore, advises: *But though we, or an angel from heaven, preach any other gospel unto you than that which we have preached unto you, let him be accursed* (Galatians 1:8).

There are enemies in the spiritual realm as there are in the physical realm. For this cause, the Holy Spirit has been given to us because He can discern spiritually. This is the reason Jesus said to His disciples: *Receive ye the Holy Ghost* (John 20:22). The Holy Spirit gives spiritual knowledge, for: *he shall teach you all things, and bring all things to your remembrance* (John 14:26).

There is much wisdom in coming to Jesus, the author and finisher of our faith (Hebrews 12:2). For when He said: *It is finished*, nothing more needed to be added. In Him is the light of true knowledge and wisdom, for Jesus said: *I am the light of the world* (John8:12); *Come unto me, all ye that labour and are heavy laden, and I will give you rest* (Matthew 11:28). He even never said to go to Peter or John or any other disciples but only: *Come unto Me*. In Him alone is our life. He knew that no other knowledge will help building His church because He alone is her author and finisher. We have no authority to change what God has designed. Be, therefore, very careful: *lest haply you even be found to fight against God* (Acts 5:39).

Spiritual wisdom, therefore, advises us to go to the mountain, and bring wood, because God says: *my house is in ruins*. It took the whole nation to build this house in Jerusalem, therefore all the churches must be united together and build the temple of God. Indeed; *The glory of this latter house shall be greater than of the former, saith the Lord of hosts* (Haggai 2:9).

# *Blow the Trumpet*

*Blow the trumpet in Zion, and sound an alarm in my holy mountain: let all the inhabitants of the land tremble: for the day of the Lord cometh, for it is nigh at hand* (Joel 2:1).

The prophet Joel faithfully conveyed this message to the nation of Israel. It is also God's word to us all.

Warnings of the Day of the Lord have been clearly given in the Scriptures. Whenever God's people became complacent, warnings always preceded the judgment. Joel was again prompted by God to repeat the warning because the situation was grave:

*Blow the trumpet in Zion, sanctify a fast, call a solemn assembly: Gather the people, sanctify the congregation, assemble the elders, gather the children, and those that suck the breasts: let the bridegroom go forth of his chamber, and the bride out of her closet. Let the priests, the ministers of the Lord, weep between the porch and the altar, and let them say, Spare thy people, O Lord, and give not thine heritage to reproach, that the heathen should rule over them: wherefore should they say among the people, Where is their God?* (Joel 2:15-17). These messages were as loud as is the trumpet sound.

Jesus on the contrary warned us saying: *do not sound a trumpet before thee, as the hypocrites do in the synagogues and in the streets, that they may have glory of men. Verily I say unto you, They have their reward* (Matthew 6:2). For when one sounds an alarm, we do for the glory of men and we get the applause of them. Such call should be to the glory of God. When we hear God's message it prepares us to stand in the Day of the Lord. Therefore, God says it is time for a solemn assembly of all God's people, elders, ministering priests, even children and newly married couples to gather. It is a trumpet call from God's holy mountain.

All priests and ministers of the Lord were told to assemble in the holy place to 'weep between the porch and the altar.' It was repentance time. The task of ministers of the Gospel does not start in earnest until they weep over their own affairs and the condition of their assemblies and should pray earnestly for God to spare His people. Repentance brings glory to all the people.

At Christ's crucifixion, the curtain of the temple was torn in two for us all to have access to the Holy of Holies. It is sad that most of us do not enter even between the porch and the altar. Call is for all believers to intercede for all people. In many ways we have misled many from God's ways. During the Babylonian captivity, Daniel wept for his people. Like Daniel, Joel and many others through the ages, we must seek the Lord to 'spare thy people.' For Jesus has lifted up His Church and wants His people to enter by the way of the cross, enter the Holy of Holies and meet His majesty.

Scriptures tell us: *The heads thereof judge for reward, and the priests thereof teach for hire, and the prophets thereof divine for money: yet will they lean upon the Lord, and say, Is not the Lord among us? None evil can come upon us.* (Micah 3:11). This was the condition of the priests that had gone to burn incense before other gods, and had led God's people astray.

During the time of exodus from Egypt; *the people brake off the golden earrings which were in their ears, and brought them unto Aaron. And he received them at their hand, and fashioned it with a graving tool, after he had made it a molten calf; and they said, These be thy gods, O Israel, which brought thee up out of the land of Egypt. And when Aaron saw it, he built an altar before it; ... And they rose up early on the morrow, and offered burnt offerings, and brought peace offerings; and the people sat down to eat and to drink, and rose up to play* (Exodus 32:3-6).

Similar conditions had prompted Joel to say: **blow the trumpet.** If these priests had been obedient to God and done what God commanded them to do, there would have been no need for calling a solemn assembly. God's people were taken to Babylon in captivity because of the complacency of the priests and Levites. They neither obeyed God nor feared Him.

God has called us to repentance. For if the very foundation of our churches be shaky, how can the structure hold? Most of the ministers of the Gospel have generally been complacent throughout the history. Where the sheep are to be tended, there are hirelings who, when they see any wolf coming, run away. It is sad that many God's sheep have become victim of the evil one.

Most shepherds today look after their own interests and glory. Many of them have big congregations. Alas! Most of them have not obeyed the trumpet call because their primary concern is about their own job, comfort, prestige, name, finances or denominational interests.

The sound of the trumpet today also is so loud that we can no longer sleep. If we remain asleep, we will surely die.

Apostle Paul writes: *For as in Adam all die, even so in Christ shall all be made alive* (1 Corinthians 15:22). Let us all leave the Adam's nature and be found alive in Christ. Jesus wants to personally guide us to the Promised Land. The time is ripe to weep for our misdoing and seek the Lord's mercies on us and our people. Once we have obeyed God and repented sincerely, God will pass over us and take us to where He is, where glory dwells forever.

He is calling us to the ocean of mercy and love. We need to be bound to Him on His cross in love.

# Conflict Within and Without

*And from the days of John the Baptist until now the kingdom of heaven suffereth violence, and the violent take it by force* (Matthew 11:12). The waves of diversity and strong winds of time have beaten upon the Church incessantly. Within the Church there have been divisions as new ideologies have crept from many directions.

Violence that began at the time of John the Baptist against Christ is still an active force within the churches. But history reveals that whenever the churches took a step of faith, they have been victorious. And whenever they turned to the world, heresies crept in and joined these disintegrating forces and weakened us. Many crusades were fought but they had also motive other than the spreading of the Gospel. But thanks be unto our Lord that, even during these Dark Ages, many remained faithful to their Master. That light still shines in this world and is due to sacrifices of such believers who exalted the Name of Jesus Christ amidst the effluents of secular thinkers.

Violence had started in the early Church. Apostle Paul says: *I beseech you, brethren, by the name of our Lord Jesus Christ, that ye all speak the same thing, and that there be no division among you; but that ye be perfectly joined together in the same mind and in the same judgment* (I Corinthians 1:10).

But this appears to have fallen on deaf ears for even now the Church is plagued by so many denominations. Most of the leaders who gave birth to these denominations would now be shocked at what we have become. Most of us have fallen short of the teachings of the Gospel and hence of the glory of God.

Higher knowledge has caused the churches to compromise with the secular ideologies and the scholars have become proud in the comfort of their administrative and many abilities. These have erected the wall of sectarianism. Superiority found its way and has replaced love of servanthood. For such times, Daniel was told to; *seal the book, even to the time of the end: many shall run to and fro,* **and knowledge shall be increased** (Daniel 12:4), for God knew then our sad estate.

We are living in the days when 'increase in knowledge' has become competitive even in the churches. This desire to attain higher knowledge has led many churches to spiritual poverty when they could have had abundance by depending on the Holy Spirit. The New Testament clearly states that 'the Holy Spirit will teach us all things,' is not considered relevant anymore as many believe everything that has to be learned is already taught in their Bible colleges or seminaries. Many have the misconception that volumes of Christian books replace the guidance of the Holy Spirit.

This lack of dependence on the Holy Spirit has led many thinkers even to doubt the existence of God. Statements in the Bible are constantly debated by theologians. Instead of paying heed to the Word of God, doubts are manufactured and multiplied by scholars. Historicity and authorship of many books of the Bible have been disputed, and theologians question whether certain texts are relevant to our age. All this is done to acquire acclaim in scholarship. Simple concepts like Jesus driving out demons from many is dismissed because many consider that even to think that demons exist is old fashioned. They surmise that such beliefs result from lack of education. Those subscribing to biblical truths are ridiculed as religious fanatics.

With arguments over many biblical truths for the acquisition of higher knowledge through diverse Christian educational institutions, it became difficult to maintain uniformity in the churches' doctrines and services. Therefore, many denominations thought it necessary to formulate their own standard for conducting affairs. Thus, in some churches, prayer books were implemented so that the entire denomination would be guided by what was established by the hierarchy and their counsel. The need to depend upon the guidance of the Holy Spirit was thus conveniently set aside. Each denomination did as it pleased to suit their ideology.

These fragmented, torn, and spiritually impoverished denominations adhered partly to the truth but their human efforts grieved the Holy Spirit. However, among them there remained a few who, like the Bereans; *received the word with all readiness of mind, and searched the scriptures daily, whether those things were so* (Acts 17:11).

In China, during the Cultural Revolution, churches were closed and great persecution came upon Christians. Believers went underground and they grew spiritually and in number because God honored their faithfulness. The loyalty of such saints was so pleasing to God that in blessing He also gave them joy amidst trials and tribulations which was the cause of their survival and multiplying.

God's Word says: *Can a woman forget her sucking child, that she should not have compassion on the son of her womb? yea, they may forget, yet will I not forget thee* (Isaiah 49:15). We should all long to be such sucking children who depend on God entirely and not on our efforts. For the Bible has said: *But we are all as an unclean thing, and all our righteousness's are as filthy rags* (Isaiah 64:6).

Only humility and loyalty to the Word of God can help us. Jesus prayed: *that they all may be one* (John17:21). When unity among the churches and love for each other comes, it will cause genuine Church growth. This dying to our ways will cause us to see His resurrection power in us. The Church in China, when everybody thought was crushed completely, they saw the power of Christ's resurrection come upon them. They not only survived, but grew enormously both in number and in the Spirit. When they 'died' they threw all their differences away and unity blossomed.

It is not too late to put away every ideology that keeps us away from each other. It is time to put off the old man clothed of pride, education or denominationalism, and put on the new man resurrected by the Holy Spirit.

In His high priestly prayer, Jesus prayed earnestly for our unity. And when He rose from the dead, He said to Mary: *I ascend unto my Father, and your Father; and to my God, and your God* (John 20:17). This was the triumphant acclamation of the work of unity between Him and God and between us and Him. He uplifted the Church to the highest height and considered no difference between His relationship with His Father and His Church. The union was complete. Why then is so little unity seen in our churches today? We have tried to build our churches on differences. There are differences between people and between denominations. Cultural superiority also exists in the churches. Have we become like the Pharisees of His time of whom Jesus said: ... *do not do ye after their works: for they say, and do not* (Matthew 23:3). These charges which were directed at the religious elite of two thousand years ago were made for like leaders of all ages.

Jesus said: A *new commandment I give unto you, That ye love one another; as I have loved you, that ye also love one another* (John 13-34). Let us all be united in Him and love each other and see His glory and blessing falling on us. He has joined us to himself on the cross.

# Prisoners Everywhere

It is said that a man was put in a prison. The prison in that land was an open-air structure with bars all around it. As he was in this prison and was looking through the iron bars, he could see people walking outside. To their amazement, he said to them: "What has happened to you that you all are in prison?" Who was in the prison and who was not?

There are many who are prisoners because they have done some wrong. They were caught, tried in a court of law, found guilty and sentenced for a period of time. If such a person is not caught, he is free. But most likely that person becomes a prisoner of his crime in his mind. Then there are people who are prisoners of their own making though they live in a free society. Many are prisoners of their habits, prisoners of love or prisoners of their actions. Those in hospital beds become victims of their circumstances. There are prisoners of war and then there are those who are prisoners outside of it. Those who think that they are not prisoners of circumstances perhaps need to examine their life deeply.

There is a great deal of truth in the tale of the man in the open-air prison who regarded those outside as prisoners. Nearly everyone is in some sort of bondage. Scriptures declare *all have sinned, and come short of the glory of God* (Romans 3:23). Apostle Paul, no doubt, included himself in this statement. Yes, he was a prisoner of many a thought and action. He was the one who zealously attempted to clean the land of all Christians. This idea had not come to him out of a vacuum. He was a Pharisee and a highly educated man of his time. He had considered himself exempt from any bondage. In one of his epistles, he described his position before meeting Jesus, as *touching the righteousness which is in the law, blameless* (Philippians 3:6).

The Bible also says: *And Saul, yet breathing out threatening and slaughter against the disciples of the Lord, went unto the high priest, And desired of him letters to Damascus to the synagogues, that if he found any of this way, whether they were men or women, he might bring them bound unto Jerusalem. (Acts 9:1-2).* Then on the way to Damascus he met Jesus and discovered that he had been guilty of most of his actions and thoughts which he had wrought against Jesus. Was he not a man who walked high in esteemed religious circles? He had even called himself, blameless. He was a prisoner of his thoughts and actions.

It was not till he met Jesus that he could say *all*, including himself, *have sinned, and come short of the glory of God* (Romans 3:23). This he discovered only when he met Jesus. It was this encounter with Jesus that made him aware of his sin that set him completely free, and the glory of God descended upon him.

It is not possible to do God's work sincerely unless we meet Jesus personally. When we meet Him, we get His strength and the gift of eternal life. Till Paul left Saul behind, all his life was empty. When we also leave our old way of thinking behind, we see the glory of God in us. Most of us are prisoners of ideologies and sophisticated knowledge and religious affairs. Saul's hatred for the Church had consumed him, but he was glad he met his redeemer who proved that Jesus is real and alive. Now he became friend of those whom he hated.

As he met Jesus he also found and wrote: *this corruptible shall have put on incorruption, then shall be brought to pass the saying that is written, Death is swallowed up in victory* (1 Corinthians 15:54). Yes, Paul's death was also swallowed up in victory when he met the One who said: *I am the way; I am the resurrection; I am the light of this world; I am Alpha and Omega.* He also understood that through all ages, there is no more death but life eternal for anyone who meets Jesus personally and does not renounce Him.

This life, which is in Christ Jesus, changes sinners to saints and sets them free. Paul was not a prisoner of religion anymore, nor did he remain a prisoner any more of earthly dictates. He was a free man in Christ Jesus. The hymn writer also confirms Paul's experiences:

*Long my imprisoned spirit lay*
*Fast bound in sin and nature's night;*
*Thine eye diffused a quickening ray,*
*I woke, the dungeon flamed with light;*
*My chains fell off, my heart was free:*
*I rose, went forth, and followed Thee.*
*Amazing love! How can it be*
*That Thou, my God, shouldst die for me.*
    *- Charles Wesley, 1707-1788*

When we encounter Jesus, the glory of His resurrection penetrates our soul. It is then that these prisoners of sin and circumstances are set free for Jesus said: Then *ye shall know the truth, and the truth shall make you free* (John 8:32). Jesus is the truth, and to know Him is life indeed. So, *If the Son therefore make you free, ye shall be free indeed* (John 8:36). Jesus also set Paul free from the bondage of hatred, religiosity and his esteemed position among the leaders of his time. Now he was walking the road on which prophets, saints and angels have trod.

The devil blinds us by saying that the way to get higher is by the ladder of honor, wealth and prestige and excellence in knowledge. Adam and Eve were likewise deceived. While the Bible says *the just shall live by his faith* (Habakkuk 2:4), the world says, 'we shall live by excellence of knowledge.' One is the spiritual approach, and the other is of the world.

Many prophets, theologians, and evangelists have been deceived by too much knowledge. The worldly way of reaching the top by acquiring higher education is used in the churches liberally. We all seem to say 'let us make us a name' as if we are competing with the world. This approach is as fast as the computer age technology is changing. In this rapid increase in the knowledge and technology, most other fields are also affected. The Scriptures rightly say: *many shall run to and fro, and knowledge shall be increased* (Daniel 12:4). With the same rapid pace, churches are hastening changes in their organizations and management to compete with each other. It has caused much grief to the Holy Spirit.it.

Man's life span on this earth is very short. Should a person live a hundred years, it is like a drop in an ocean compared to eternity. Even *the days of Methuselah* (who lived longest) *were nine hundred sixty and nine* *years: **and he died** (Genesis 5:27). But life is not short. It is eternal. This has been dealt more fully in my book *Splendour For Ever*.

We must get rid of chains that have kept us bound for we are glory bound. The only way to freedom is through Christ because He alone gives the more abundant life (John 10:10) here and beyond.

God in the Old Testament is called: "the God of Abraham, Isaac and Jacob." These three great persons were different, for in each one of them God was unique but they followed God faithfully, God's blessings came upon them. To each one, God's leading came differently. These blessings were also to flow all their generations to come. However, whenever Israel disobeyed God's commands, blessings turned into curses. Similarly, for all believers, God has reserved His blessings in an infinite fashion. God just expect us all to be faithful.

Similarly, there are three types of people on this earth: sinners; believers, and the shepherds. God wants us all to be faithful like Abraham, Isaac and Jacob and be of one in mind with Him — *Let this mind be in you, which was also in Christ Jesus* (Philippians 2:5).

**Sinners:** God's love for mankind was so great that He Himself also came to this world and His love for mankind has no parallel. In loving us, He not only died to buy our redemption, but rose again and left us the good news message of salvation and eternal life — *For God so loved the world, that he gave his only begotten Son, that whosoever believeth in him should not perish, but have everlasting life* (John 3:16).

**Believers:** are the apple of His eyes. Therefore, God wants them to be like their Redeemer. Therefore Jesus says: *Let your light so shine before men, that they may see your good works, and glorify your Father which is in heaven* (Matthew 5:16). It is also His great desire that they be obedient to Him and love each other. He provides truths for believers' life style, conduct, vocation, commission, and worship.

**Shepherds:** There are many shepherds mentioned in the Bible like Moses, David and many more. Then there were shepherds who did not feed the flock of God. Very few books are written on this subject. Many instructions in the Bible are not fearfully followed by most. Perhaps because it is considered that Bible colleges and seminaries cover the subject fully. Since we are dealing with churches generally, perhaps it is proper to study these messages a little and determine the mind of God.

The Old Testament states: *Thus saith the Lord my God; Feed the flock of the slaughter; Whose possessors slay them, and hold themselves not guilty: and their own shepherds pity them not.* (Zechariah 11:4-5). The New Testament also records: *Jesus went up to Jerusalem, And found in the temple those that sold, ... when he had made a scourage of small cords, he drove them all out of the temple ... And said unto them that sold doves, Take these things hence; make not my Father's house an* **house of merchandise** (John 2:13-16). These Scripture verses tell us that there are shepherds who are selfish. They have sold the flock of God for their own good. Our Lord, by washing His disciples' feet, showed us that He came as a servant, and that all believers, which includes the ministers, should likewise serve others. However, most shepherds lord over their flock as if they are superior beings. The primary purpose of the shepherds is that the flock must be fed. If they are not fed by these shepherds, God says: *I will feed the flock of slaughter, even you, O poor of the flock* (Zechariah 11:7). We notice that God observes it all and says especially to the shepherds that if the keepers do not care for their sheep, He will have mercy upon the poor of the flock, but everyone and the shepherds are accountable to God for their disregard of His instructions.

Looking at this pathetic condition, God says: *Three shepherds also I cut off in one month; and my soul loathed them, and their soul also abhorred me* (Zechariah 11:8). This message also applies to shepherds of all ages. They have not cared enough for the flock under their care. Although the poor of the flock are fed by God the Holy Spirit, the shepherds are still answerable to God. Jesus Christ, the Chief Shepherd, has come to seek that which was lost and feed the poor of the flock and He commands us: *Feed my sheep* (John 21:17). Why should we be cut off? He simply wants us do what He did. Perhaps most of us are prisoners of our own ideologies, philosophy or denominational theology. The Bible says: *Behold, I set before you this day a blessing and a curse; A blessing, if ye obey the commandments of the Lord your God, which I command you this day: And a curse, if ye will not obey the commandments of the Lord your God, but turn aside of the way which I command you* (Deuteronomy 11:26-28).

Some shepherds, who do not know Christ personally, find it difficult to feed the flock of God. Therefore, they cannot tell their congregation much about Him. However, when a member of that flock finds Christ the Chief Shepherd, it does not please these shepherds. They do not understand that as the deer pants after the water, these members also went in search of the living water—Jesus. They had waited upon the Lord and the Holy Spirit had directed them to an oasis where they drink from the fountain head. They eat spiritual food. Sadly, because of their migration to these pastures, these saints are labeled as 'church hoppers.'

May it be soberly considered that only those who have life can hop? They hop out because they were released from their bondage. *But they that wait upon the Lord shall renew their strength; they shall mount up with wings as eagles; they shall run, and not be weary; and they shall walk, and not faint* (Isaiah 40:31). Is it not time for all shepherds to meet the Chief Shepherd first and then to follow Him? For every shepherd who knows the Chief Shepherd finds oasis of love and also let his flock drink from that fountain. For him, it becomes joy to introduce people to this Friend and set them free.

Jesus told Peter in the presence of all His disciples: 'feed my sheep/lambs (John 21:15-17). He said it three times because it was the most important thing and He said just before His ascension. But such carelessness has made many to remain prisoners of their efforts. These have remained void of God's many blessings. Going to Jesus and meeting Him is really oasis in the desert for all travelers of time. For Jesus in His love, has bound us on His cross and wants us to be with Him forever.

# Results of Fear

Fear is a force that the enemy uses to prevent mankind from progressing physically, mentally and spiritually. It is a deterrent to our advancement and is the root of man's many ailments. Armies confronted with fear have retreated and lost all they had. In the shadow of fear many empires have disappeared. It has taken people to darkness even when light was knocking at their door.

The fear is in the spirit realm and is called 'spirit of fear.' It affects our mind and nervous system. And when the nervous system is affected, resistance to disease becomes weak. The 'spirit of fear' is demonic and it affects the individual's joy and serenity. Being demonic, it becomes active at the spiritual level also and affects us physically, mentally and spiritually. The Bible teaches us that: *God hath not given us the spirit of fear; but of power, and of love, and of a sound mind* (II Timothy 1:7).

**Evaporation of Fear**

Whenever a person had a heavenly visitation and saw an angel of the Lord, they were first frightened. Could it be because of the interference of the devil? But, in almost every instance, the angel's first words were 'Do not be afraid.' As soon as these words were heard, calm prevailed and heavenly communication was well received. In the presence of God and His Word, there is joy, love, a sound mind, and perfect peace prevail. To testify the disappearance of fear in the presence of God, I relate a personal experience.

## My Testimony

In November 1952, I was a young man in a bus going on a weekend vacation to a mountain village nestled in the foothills of the Himalayan Mountains in India. The bus stopped in a small town, Kangra, because night driving on this mountainous road was extremely unsafe. I decided to proceed on foot to my sister's house which was a little more than three miles by a short cut from Kangra. I had earlier traveled this route as a child. I had a blanket and a small suitcase with me.

Although I knew that this terrain was never travelled by anyone at night, I tried to engage a porter to take my brief case just for company. When I told him that I wanted to go to Tanda, he refused to go. I offered him ten times the wage he would get for carrying a heavy load during the day, but he said: "if it is Tanda, even if you give me that much or much more, I will not go." I received the same reply from another coolie.

Then I decided to proceed alone. I had a flash light, but the cells in it were so weak it would hardly give any light. I went to buy new cells but all the shops had closed by that time. I therefore decided to conserve the light using it sparingly. I would flash the flash light for a second attempting to cover as much distance as possible. Having some knowledge of the territory, I knew that I would not find a single person after walking past a dozen houses.

There was a house which I knew was haunted. I passed it. Then there was a big tree in the middle of the road which was an idol worship center during day and was famous for being haunted. I passed it also. Now there lay before me a solitary trail winding through the bushes, trees, steep hills and sometimes over slippery stone steps. I reached a point where that path would lead me down a steep hill. Thick mango trees on both sides of the track made visibility very poor and the stone steps covered with these trees' sap were slippery. At the bottom of this hill, there was an open cremation ground on one side. After it, a bridge spanned over a river. While I was crossing the bridge, I saw a fire glowing in the bed rocks of the river. Since the cremation ground was nearby, I thought the fire was of glowing bones. At this time, I was merrily singing hymns –

> *Abide with me: fast falls the even tide;*
> *The darkness deepens; Lord with me abide!*

> *When other helpers fail, and comforts flee,*
> *Help of the helpless, O abide with me*
> *- Henry F. Lyte, 1793-1847.*

As I crossed the narrow bridge, the path led through a plateau, after which it would wind up another mountain beyond which was my destination. Because it was almost winter, it was common for wild animals, like panthers and tigers, to come down to the lower mountains. This valley was also notorious for poisonous snakes. As I stepped into this plateau, there was an open ground for a few yards, and I was singing the hymn - by Isaac Watts (1674-1748):

> *When I survey the wondrous cross,*
> *On which the Prince of Glory died,*
> *My richest gain I count but loss,*
> *And pour contempt on all my pride.*

I knew all its four verses by heart. I still had a distance of at least a mile and a half to cover.

When I was singing its third verse:

> *See, from His head, His hands, His feet,*
> *Sorrow and love flow mingled down;*
> *Did e'er such love and sorrow meet,*
> *Or thorns compose so rich a crown?*

to my great delight, I saw two amazingly beautiful feet on my right side walking with me. These feet had a very soft glow. Immediately, I realized that it was my Jesus who was walking with me. I had peace, but now perfect peace descended on me seeing that He was with me. I did not even look upon Him but promptly leaned on Him, put all my weight on Him and completely lost myself in the comfort of His presence. (It reminded me that John, the disciple of the Lord, used to lean on Jesus.)

Next thing I remember I was only about one hundred yards from my destination. I certainly did not walk the mile and a half after meeting Jesus. I most certainly was transported in His loving arms. There must have been danger ahead of me when He came to help me. When Jesus is there, all fear is gone for who can harm a child of God?

When I mentioned this episode to the inhabitants of the district, I discovered that there was only one other person who had travelled that path at night and that was thirty-two years prior to this event. This person was my father, Duni Chand, who had on many occasions met Jesus personally. He was called home at the age of 107. His memoirs can be viewed at the website: www.weatjesusfeet.blogspot.ca under the title - My Shepherd for the Third Century.

The bus arriving late and stopping for the night in Kangra; not getting any coolie to escort me; my determination to walk alone, was all in God's plan. May I say that "Jesus had an appointment to meet me and I did not know it." He surely came to assure that no harm would fall on me. He taught me, through this episode that **in His presence there is no fear.** When I saw His feet which were so glorious, how much more gorgeous could it be if I saw Him? No harm, demons or any power could touch those who call upon Him. His beautiful softly glowing feet will guide us, He will lift us and take us to our desired destination.

In the presence of God, fear disappears and the perfect peace that passeth understanding becomes ours.

## Fear of God

There are numerous references in the Old Testament that emphasize that God is to be feared. There is, however a great difference between the 'spirit of fear' and the 'fear of God.' King Solomon wrote: *The fear of the Lord is the beginning of wisdom* (Proverbs 9:10). The 'spirit of fear' causes a barrier to keep us away from God. The Bible also says: *The hand of our God is upon all them for good that seek him; but his power and his wrath is against all them that forsake him* (Ezra 8:22). And Paul says: *For the wrath of God is revealed from heaven against all ungodliness and unrighteousness of men, who hold the truth in unrighteousness* (Romans 1:18).

But the fear of God is our refuge. It also causes one to turn to God. Therefore, when fear of God descends upon such persons and they turn to God knowing that God's wrath will come upon those who do not fear Him, they become children of God guided by His Spirit and the fear is replaced with the love of God. They are no longer in condemnation because their sins are not remembered anymore. To them, God instantly becomes a loving Shepherd, and His sheep find green pastures.

These sheep must continue following their Shepherd. Should they fall and repent, Jesus' loving arms are always stretched to embrace them again.

Fear of God comes when we do anything contrary to the will of God. In the Garden of Eden, God called Adam when they had sinned, Adam's answer to God was: *I heard thy voice in the garden, and **I was afraid** because I was naked; and I hid myself* (Genesis 3:10). Saint Paul also admonishes us to *work out your own salvation **with fear** and trembling* (Philippians 2:12). Fear and trembling before God leads us to repentance and fellowship with Him. If there is anyone to be feared, no clearer direction could be found than that which came from our Lord himself who said: *But I will forewarn you whom ye shall fear: Fear him, which after he hath killed hath power to cast into hell; **yea, I say unto you, Fear him*** (Luke 12:5). We are surely counselled to fear God. Fear of God is holy and is to be revered. Therefore, whatever we do, if we have the fear of God, we will be blessed.

## Fear in Worship

Lord Jesus also taught us that *the true worshippers shall worship the Father in spirit and in truth: for the Father seeketh such to worship him* (John 4:23). When we worship Him: *He will fulfil the desire of them that fear him: he also will hear their cry, and will save them* (Psalm 145:19).

Our God is holy. We cannot offer Him strange worship. *Nadab and Abihu died before the Lord, when they offered strange fire before the Lord, in the wilderness of Sinai, and they had no children* (Numbers 3:4). To worship Him in truth and spirit, the Bible also says: *work out your own salvation with fear and trembling* (Philippians 2:12). If our worship is designed to entertain, then we do not have the fear of God. Only true worship will lead us to the throne of grace which fill us with joy unspeakable and will also enable us to see His glory in the comfort of His love. Jesus has admonished us to: *Fear him* (Luke 12:5). For when our worship of Him is in spirit and in truth, He joins us because He so seeks. Then our worship of Him becomes the fragrance of His love and presence.

The love of God flows so much in the New Testament that Jesus commanded us to love one another. For Jesus Christ is the fountain of love too. The Old Testament speaks of Messiah so much and the New Testament tells us: *Jesus Christ the same yesterday, and to day, and for ever* (Hebrews 13:8). Christ, who walks in the pages of the Scriptures, does not change to tell us to love one another.

God so loved the world that He was manifested in the flesh. The source of all love which was hidden in the Old Testament has become our lover. However the fact that God is to be feared remains intact in the New Testament. But those who do not believe in Him are condemned already.

Condemnation is the result of God's judgment and is to be greatly feared. But in the love of Jesus, those who believe in Him, His gift is eternal life with Him.

The New Testament complements the Old Testament. Therefore, the God of the Old Testament who was to be feared is also the God of the New Testament to be feared. Because He never changes, New Testament has displayed Agape love in human flesh, but it does not change any facts of the Old Testament concerning the nature of God.

The messages to the seven churches in the Book of Revelation warn saints of the judgments of God. The theology that God in His love is going to forgive everybody does not agree with the Word of God. The Scriptures say: *it is appointed unto men once to die, but after this the judgment* (Hebrews 9:27). God is just and we are going to face His righteous judgement. Hebrews 10:31 states: *It is a fearful thing to fall into the hands of the living God.* He does not want anyone to perish but to be saved. Therefore, Jesus said, *Fear Him.* (Luke 12:5).

He is also a loving God for those whose conduct is right in His sight, though they be ridiculed by the world. Therefore, when we draw close to Him, fear and trembling is replaced by rejoicing in His mercies and love.

## No Fear in Obedience

Then there is a fear which leads to repentance. King Solomon said: *it shall be well with them that fear God, which fear before him* (Ecclesiastes 8:12). Fear of God leads us to the goodness of the Lord, and *the goodness of God leadeth thee to repentance* (Romans 2:4). Fear of God is good because every time fear strikes, the fear of the Lord takes us to the throne of Grace where we find mercy.

Whenever we sin, our hearts convict us just like David's heart was much grieved when he sinned. He had then found that the joy he had of his salvation was gone and that he was unclean before God. Therefore, he prayed for God's mercies to: *blot out my transgressions. Wash me thoroughly from mine iniquity, and cleanse me from my sin* (Psalm 51:1-2). He opened his heart to the Lord and sought Him saying: *Restore unto me the joy of thy salvation* (Psalm 51:12). The fear of God had brought him back to God and the joy of salvation was restored to him.

The fear of the Lord indeed makes us wise to turn to the author and finisher of our faith. Any time David was in turmoil or when he was confronted with an enemy, it was another opportunity for him to come back to his maker.

When fear strikes, we must return to our God for wisdom. In God's presence, there is no fear, and in the absence of fear there are no barriers between us and the Lord. Shadrach, Meshach and Abed-nego had no fear when they told king Nebuchadnezzar: *we are not careful to answer thee in this matter. If it be so, our God whom we serve is able to deliver us from the burning fiery furnace, and he will deliver us out of thine hand, O king* (Daniel 3:16-17).

Daniel was thrown in the lions' den at King Nebuchadnezzar's command. It seems he had no fear. On the other hand, the hungry lions in that den had fear of God because of the presence of a real servant of God.

When our relationship with our God is unwavering, fear of lions or fiery furnaces or anything else has no place. It all depends on our trust in Him.

## The Great Commission and Fear

The Bible says: *the kingdom of heaven suffereth violence, and the violent take it by force* (Matthew 11:12). Christianity has suffered continued attacks from the enemy because fear is devil's grip with which he attacks us. This fear has been dominant in most churches with the result that obedience to God has been replaced with disobedience. There is also so much fear especially when praying for the sick and laying hands on the sick.

The fear of the world is destructive to our body, soul and spirit. With our much learning and rational mind, logic has much replaced obedience to God. Doctrines in the churches are also often geared to fit modern social concepts which are changing our values and have watered down the standards of faith.

We thank God for those faithful few, though not much respected by most churches, have sought God with all their heart. They are a minority like Noah who: *found grace in the eyes of the Lord* (Genesis 6:8).

It is sad that instead of preaching the pure Word, most endeavor to preach philosophy, doctrines, denominational theology and cultural misdemeanours, all mingled with the Word. Wisdom calls to be wise in God for the things of this word are temporary.

## Evangelism

Many churches give priority to evangelism. There are training courses for those desiring to go into the world to be fishers of men. It is a common misconception that teachers or ministers are the only people adequately trained to impart the saving grace of our Lord, since they have spent much time studying. Lay persons who do not have such educational background and do not have a certificate or degree in theology are somehow not deemed fit for the task for such credentials are considered the requisite to evangelize.

In some evangelical churches, there is also a program called 'friendship evangelism.' It enables those who have not undertaken a course in evangelism to bring their unsaved friends to the church. Then the pastor will impart Gospel knowledge to them.

Many Christian educational institutions have developed these programs with great care. The need to depend upon the Holy Spirit is thus not considered paramount because their main emphasis is on human efforts. Have our biblical institutions indeed become so sophisticated that we do not need the assistance of the Holy Spirit? We cannot replace the teaching of the Holy Spirit, for grieving Him, we will fall.

New theologies have made inroads in almost every phase of our churches and the Holy Spirit has little place in worshipping God. When Jesus said: *the Comforter, which is the Holy Ghost, whom the Father will send in my name,* **he shall teach you all things, and bring all things to your remembrance, whatsoever I have said unto you** (John 14:26) has no regard. If we negate the need and the role of the Holy Spirit in our lives, are we the body of Christ? Jesus also said: *All manner of sin and blasphemy shall be forgiven unto men: but the blasphemy against the Holy Ghost shall* *not be forgiven unto men. And whosoever speaketh a word against the Son of man, it shall be forgiven him: but whosoever speaketh against the Holy Ghost, it shall not be forgiven him, neither in this world, neither in the world to come* (Matthew 12:31-32).

## Preachers' Dilemma

Over the years, preaching has become very articulate. There are courses on the art of preaching and homiletics and like subjects are pursued by most. Such methods are greatly valued as they enhance the delivery of the message. Hence systematic techniques are greatly in use. Also, generally the scholarly preaching has become a product of philosophy and theology. When our minds are focused on such techniques and excellence of exposition, we naturally tend to pay less attention to His leading. Our mind ought to be led by the Holy Spirit realizing that there are people who are hungry and thirsty for simple Word of God. The Scriptures state: *The tongue of the sucking child cleaveth to the roof of his mouth for thirst: the young children ask bread, and no man breaketh it unto them* (Lamentations 4:4).

Simple preaching comes with the help of the Holy Spirit and bears much fruit. The Church of the first century triumphed because of simple preaching.

## Fear in the Churches

A shift of population is often affected by economic conditions. Families move from one area of a city or country to another for many reasons. This movement affects attendance in some churches. Whenever attendance decreases in a church, it becomes a cause of great concern. Such like conditions made the early Church to go everywhere and more churches were established as their motive was to honor God.

People emigrate from a church because they are spiritually hungry. If they are not fully fed, naturally their spiritual hunger will take them to another place. At times, the Holy Spirit also guides them in this. The spirit of a man is aware of the fact that unless he can be one with the Spirit of God, there is great danger ahead of them. For, *The spirit of man is the candle of the Lord, searching all the inward parts of the belly* (or heart) (Proverbs

20:27). The Holy Spirit is that lamp which feeds them. The Bible says: *they shall all be taught by God* (John 6:45). In such circumstances, it is the Holy Spirit that takes a child of God to a place where they can find oasis and are fed manna.

Often when the congregation starts dwindling in a church, fear seems to grip the elite. Spirit of fear, as we studied earlier, is not from God. It is evil. Should fear strike, it must be dealt with at the spiritual level. At such times, it is necessary for the leaders of the church to unload their burden at the foot of the cross, examine the situation in the light of God's Word, and seek His help and direction. As we return to the Lord and commit our lives and ways once again to serve Him faithfully according to His blueprint, the Lord will be gracious to us and in the midst of unforeseen hardships, He will lead along the right and glorious path.

The church that belongs to God must function as the Lord wants for it is bought by the blood of Jesus Christ. The full price for it has already been paid and she is the property of God. Therefore, everybody should commit themselves to the Lord and also commit all their ministries to God as well because we are His ministers. All in the church need the hands of the Lord who is the Chief Shepherd. The Church is a spiritual body. As long as it has human efforts, it has little spiritual blessing. Jesus himself said: *God is a Spirit: and they that worship him must worship him in spirit and in truth* (John 4:24).

Churches throughout history have erected monumental buildings, cathedrals and empires. Like Nimrod, most churches want to leave behind their name upon this earth. They are busy building towers whose height they expect would reach unto heaven. It did not work for Nimrod and it will not work for us. But much effort still continues to be exerted in trying to build monumental organizations, denominations and ministries. The Tower of Babel stood uncompleted, and so will any human effort remain incomplete because we intend to build a spiritual building using physical efforts.

The Bible says: *For where your treasure is, there will your heart be also* (Matthew 6:21). If our treasures are in the earthly organizations and efforts, how can we expect to have any treasure in heaven? Therefore: *Awake thou that sleepest, and arise from the dead, and Christ shall give thee light* (Ephesians 5:14).

What a Friend we have who has bound us in love eternally.

# His Own

An Old Testament prophet writes: *And one shall say unto him, What are these wounds in thine hands? Then he shall answer, Those with which I was wounded in the house of my friends* (Zechariah 13:6). When Christ the Messiah came, the Jewish authorities rejected and crucified Him. However, death and the tomb could not keep Him. At His resurrection, He said to His disciples: *Why are you troubled? And why do thoughts arise in your hearts? Behold my hands and my feet, that it is I myself: handle me and see; for a spirit hath not flesh and bones, as ye see me have* (Luke 24:38-39). Yes, He indeed was tortured in the house of His friends. His own disciple reports: *He* (Jesus) *came unto his own, and his own received him not* (John 1:11).

We have the knowledge of all Scriptures with us. We know that: *He is despised and rejected of men; a man of sorrows, and acquainted with grief: ... he was bruised for our iniquities; the chastisement of our peace was upon him* (Isaiah 53:3,5). However, when we hear the words of our Lord spoken to the scribes and Pharisees: *Woe unto you, scribes and Pharisees, hypocrites! because ye build the tombs of the prophets, and garnish the sepulchres of the righteous, And say, If we had been in the days of our fathers, we would not have been partakers with them in the blood of the prophets. Wherefore ye be witnesses unto yourselves, that ye are the children of them which killed the prophets* (Matthew 23:29-31), we wonder if He was also speaking to us.

Yes, we also have rejected Him. We have betrayed Him by not acknowledging who He is. Betrayal is as bad as treason. Jesus said: *woe unto that man by whom the Son of man is betrayed* (Matthew 26:24). However,

He said: *Whosoever therefore shall confess me before men, him will I confess also before my Father which is in heaven* (Matthew 10:32).

When Jesus instituted the sacrament of the Holy Communion, He did it among his friends and disciples. These were His elected. It was at this occasion that He said: *He that dippeth his hand with me in the dish, the same shall betray me* (Matthew 26:23). *And they were exceeding sorrowful, and began every one of them to say unto him, Lord, is it I?* (Matthew 26:22). Though Jesus was their Master, most of them denied Him by running away that very night. Is it not befitting for all believers and shepherds today to ask the same question to themselves, is it Me?

> *Betrayed by my own, whom I chose to be my disciple;*
> *Woe unto him; better if he had never been born.*
> *How often we betray Him and ask Him the question,*
> *Master, Is it I, Is it me, O Lord?*
>
> *Betrayal is not esteemed on earth or in heaven,*
> *Though we have walked with Jesus all our life long.*
> *So, next time, my friend, when you remember the Lord,*
> *Ask, IS IT ME, O LORD, your friend or betrayer?*

Yes, we have also betrayed Him sometime or the other, especially by not obeying His commands. We have disregarded the Great Commission. When we have tried to fulfill it, we have done it only partly. We delight to seek direction from our hierarchy or take a democratic approach in our general and board meetings to arrive at a majority decision or general consensus. At Jesus' trial, the general consensus shouted: *Crucify Him, Crucify Him (Luke23:21).*

At that gathering, if there were some who had said 'No' to His crucifixion, their voices were drowned in pursuit of democratic principles—democracy prevailed. Though we are grateful that He was crucified, be it known that general consensus is not always right. Today also, such small voices are drowned. Even the voice of the Holy Spirit is drowned by general consensus by denominational directives and many such acts. If sadly He asked the question to Peter in the presence of other disciples, "Do you love me", He says today to us all, Feed my sheep/lambs (John 21:15-17). He said three times because it was the most important thing. If we are not faithful to feed His sheep, will He give us His blessing in our running of His affairs?

*But as many as received him, to them gave he power to become the sons of God, even to them that believe on his name* (John 1:12). When we call ourselves children of God, it is of utmost importance that we do what He says. We might think that we are His, but when it comes to doing His will, we do only a small part of what He told us to do. Should we not do exactly what He says so that we can become His own and rightly be called His children?

In the Great Commission, He has left His heart's desire for us and has also equipped us with divine authority. He came to this earth; He suffered, died, rose again and now is sitting at the right hand of God. He also wants us to be at His right hand when the sheep will be separated from the goats. It is profitable for us, therefore, to fulfilling His Great three-fold Commission earnestly – He went, He preached and healed all who came to Him (Matthew 4:23). He commanded us to do, go, teach and heal saying: *The works that I do shall he do also* (John 14:12). Our mission is therefore to go, teach and heal also. This is His command to us. We Christians have gone everywhere, taught the Word, but healing is not considered much important which He has purposed. No human knowledge, education or technology can substitute what He has ordained. God's ways are much higher compared to our wisdom or any of our esteemed abilities and human efforts.

Jesus has bound us with Him on His cross in love because one wood of the cross was His and the second was ours. Also, when He had said: *It is finished* (John 19:30), our works has started of fulfilling the Great Commission.

# Vision of Victory

The world of dreams is as big as are the stars in the sky or sand on the sea. Everybody dreams not only when asleep but every day. Some of the dreams are what one wishes to be real. Most dreams are forgotten, but some that are remembered may or can be significant. Because we are both physical and spiritual beings, the world of dreams and of visions cover both the worlds for there we behold things that are seen and unseen. Historically also, such dreams and visions have made great impact on the affairs of this world. Some of these are inspired by God and these are the ones which we ought to consider seriously. God has often warned mankind through dreams and visions of many coming disastrous and also of things of great value to mankind.

It was the end of February, 2018, when I had an unusual dream. It was not a pleasant one and my mind was not at rest seeing it; but it had a shout of victory at the end. Therefore, I was determined to find its interpretation. Very soon I discovered that it was meant for the whole Church at large which has often been struggling hard to be victorious in this world.

I have never liked snakes for the very mention of it was always disgusting to me. In this dream, or vision, I saw a very big snake which was about six feet long. Its entire body was crumbled but its head was still alive and was still hurting people. I had an old butcher knife in my right hand which was about 18 inches long and had a wooden handle. Its blade was about four inches deep and at its sharp end it was about seven inches. I saw this beast on my right while I was sitting on the floor and was about two feet away from the beast. I took this knife and with one blow slit the head of the beast so that the knife split its entire head, right in the middle from its all-crumbled part to its mouth, the part that was still alive. I had no fear of the beast though I was on the floor so close to it. I had also no hesitation to do what I did.

When I was discussing this dream with other believers, we discovered that it was not any different from the episode mentioned in the book of Genesis which states: *And the Lord God said unto the serpent, Because thou hast done this … I will put enmity between thee and the woman, and between thy seed and her seed; it shall bruise thy head, and thou shalt bruise his heel* (Genesis 3:14-15). Now there was no doubt that God was sending a message to the churches.

The Church, throughout history, has been victimized by the works of the devil though she, by God's help, has been overcoming. But the enemy activity is still hurting people.

Jesus had fought the battle of the centuries at the cross and defeated all the works of the devil. Then, at His resurrection: *he breathed on them, and saith unto them* (His disciples), *Receive ye the Holy Ghost* (John 20:22) and gave them the power saying: *tarry ye in the city of Jerusalem, until ye be endued with power from high* (Luke 24:49). He had also earlier told them: *the works that I do shall he do also; and **greater works** than these shall he do; because I go unto my Father* (John14:12). The Church is the body of Christ and is expected to do great works. But the head of the beast that I saw was still active to bruise. Is it not for the Church to crush the beast's head?

But the church has lost its full potential because of its splits and fragmentation. While the Spirit of the Lord is anxious that she should be strong, the divisions in her have grieved Him and, like Samson, her strength in the Lord has depleted. We have become weak because of such divisions. The Bible encourages us and says: *Strengthen ye the weak hands, and confirm the feeble knees* (Isaiah 35:3). Therefore, we are called to put on the **whole** armor of God and: *bruise thy* (the serpent) *head*. The battle sometime seems to be too strong, but God says: *Be not afraid … for the battle is not your's, but God's* (2 Chronicles 20:15). And when Jesus says: *lo, I am with you alway* (Matthew 28:20), surely, He wants to joins us and fight all our battles. The victory is always on the way when we are obeying the Victor. Knowing that His followers will not always heed to Him completely, Jesus earnestly prayed: *that they all may be one* (John 17:21). Unity among the brethren has been greatly emphasized in the Scriptures because in unity there is strength. If we cannot love the ones we see, how can we love God whom we have not seen. Unity with our Lord and with His children is the key to our victory. By divisions among ourselves, we have become weak. Therefore: *taking the shield of faith, wherewith ye shall be able to quench all the fiery darts of the wicked* (Ephesians 6:16); for the fiery darts are the ones with which the devil still is active to hurt the Church. Though many of us are enjoying the blessings from above, till we are all united, we remain short of His glory.

In His great love for mankind, Jesus, like Moses, gave us the commandment: *Thou shalt love the Lord thy God with all thy heart, and with all thy soul, and with all thy mind … Thou shalt love thy neighbor as thyself* (Matthew 22:37,39). In this two-fold command, love demands unity with God and with our neighbor. For where there is unity, there is love, strength, joy, peace and power. Apostle Paul also writes in 1 Corinthians 13:13: *And now abideth faith, hope, Charity, these three; but the greatest of these is charity* (love). Jesus is that fountain of love and whosoever shall drink of that fountain shall never thirst again. Therefore, to have that love, Jesus says: *This is my commandment: That ye love one another, as I have loved you* (John 15:12). In love there is such great power that even to pray for those who hate us, it is sheer joy that fills our heart with peace that knows no end. It brings the joy of heaven down to earth and also causes many to see and enter the kingdom where love has no bounds.

In the vision, the knife's handle in my right hand was made of wood. The sharp seven-inch steel knife used to split the head of the beast represented the mighty power of God in the Church's hand; while the wooden handle represents the strength of the wooden cross. These both are needed to overcome the adversary of our soul and spirit. We all need be one in the hand of our God only then we will hear the trumpet sound of victory. The wall of our diversity will come down when we all are united as one in the hand of God, and will shout victory over the enemy.

Though I was sitting so close to the beast, I had no fear of it but had strength and wisdom to do what I did. It is always being one in the hand of the Lord that wisdom and strength comes to fight even the ancient serpent, the enemy of our soul, spirit and body, who had visited Adam and Eve and trodden down the sacred empire of the Garden of Eden. He simply wants us to be strong in His might. In the battles that Jesus fought with the forces of the devil, Jesus crushed the enemy, and in the Great Commission, He has commissioned the Church to do the same. For He had said: *the works that I do shall he do also; and greater works than these shall he do* (John 14:12). This battle where the devil has power to hurt the saints, and even over death, will be completely crushed by one blow of the Church united when we are one with Him and with each other. Victory over the enemy is as close as when we get in one accord around our Lord. Jesus has said: *my peace I give unto you; not as the world giveth, give I unto you. Let not your heart be trouble, neither let it be afraid* (John 14:27). We will have a good bon fire of victory and peace for in unity our enemy will have been defeated as miracles take place.

As the Bible says: *And I will put enmity between thee and the woman, and between thy seed and her seed; it shall bruise thy head, and thou shall bruise his heel* (Genesis 3:15). Jesus indeed has bruised the enemy's head. Now He says to His Children, the Church: *He that believeth on me, the works that I do shall he do also; and greater works than these shall he do; because I go unto my Father,* the greater work is to completely split the head of the snake already bruised. The Bible encourages us to: *Fight the good fight of* faith (1 Timothy 6:12). Since faith can move the mountains, and when we all are united, the battle belongs to our God. Jesus bruised Satan's head; His bride, the Church, which has been given all power, must also crush his head. O Church, Jesus has said: *I give unto you power to tread on serpents and scorpions, and over all the power of the enemy; and nothing shall by any means hurt you* (Luke 10:19). We can hear the bells of victory.

David, the man after God's heart, writes: *Behold, how good and how pleasant it is for brethren to dwell together in unity* (Psalm 133:1). His union with God also caused God to give him the kingdom over Judah and Israel. Therefore, He is also called sweet psalmist because his song was, the Lord is my shepherd. The Unity among the churches is also vitally important irrespective of all manmade differences. It is vital because the Bible says: *For we wrestle not against flesh and blood, but against principalities, against power, against the rulers of darkness of this world, against spiritual wickedness in high places*, and advises: *Wherefore take unto you the whole armor of God* (Ephesians 6:12-13). The cross of Jesus is our armor for where one piece of the cross is His and the other is ours. That is where our strength lies. The vertical piece points to heaven from where comes our help; and when we join ourselves to Him as one, we have the help from above. The horizontal piece of the cross belonged to mankind, and it demands our relationship with mankind to be worthy of the Cross. When our relationship with Christ and each other is solid, union is real. Who can separate us from such union, for in this union, our victory is assured? We shall surely fight the good fight of faith and shall be able to say: *Death is swallowed up in victory. O death, where is thy sting? … But thanks be to God which giveth us the victory through our Lord Jesus Christ* (1 Corinthians 15:54-57)?

**Evangelism and healing** are the fragrance of heaven on earth and was the ministry of our Lord, Jesus Christ. For He said: *Believe me that I am in the Father, and the Father in me; or else believe me for the very works' sake* (John 14:11). If Jesus had to prove His ministry through His works, how much more we need to follow His example. In countries where revivals have taken place, people have also been convicted because of the healing and miracles, and there have been mass conversions to Christianity. It is the sword of the spirit that brings the victory, and is not any different than using the seven inches knife of our faith. It is this victory that the devil is afraid of and is causing the division in the body of Christ. Faith and obedience are the weapons of our warfare which crush all powers of our enemy, both in the physical and spiritual realms. The Church's one purpose is to stand and fight the good fight of faith and overcome. This victory is glorious for the Church for when the life ends on this earth, the portals of heaven are open wide for her. Evangelism and healing are what the devil and his hoard hates. And it is the evangelism and healing that is the weapon against the forces of the devil and his kingdom. It can only be used by the Church for it is the weapon in our hand. As we approach the end time, let the Church be strong, fight the battles of the Lord, for we must not be afraid of the devil. The Lord is with us. He has given us the power and authority over all the works of the enemy. With these weapons in our hand, the head of beast will be split as was revealed in the vision with the knife.

The Church is the powerhouse of God on earth and is the glory of God. Because Jesus has overcome death, the Church victory is assured over the works of the devil. Jesus is the Victor and those who believe on Him must be victorious. The secret of His being victorious is that: *God so loved the world, that he gave his only begotten Son, that whosoever believeth in him should not perish, but have everlasting life* (John 3:16). His love for humanity is victory tool indeed. It is His love that invites us all, saying: *Come unto me, all ye that labour and are heavy laden, and I will give you rest* (Matthew 11:28). In His death and resurrection is our victory for He has already gained the victory for us and will fight all our battles too in order to make us victorious like Him. He has, therefore, given us the authority over all the works of the devil to cast out all demonic forces. And by this authority and in His name, people are also healed of all diseases, and even dead are raised to life. In healing, it is the virtue of God that eliminates the darkness and all fear that has invaded mankind, for such are the weapon which the enemy has ever used. Praise God, there is sound of victory everywhere.

The wisdom says, get hold of the power of God and take the sword of the Spirit. In unity with Jesus and with each other, we shall prevail against all the works of Satan. For when we walk thus, we only see the banner of victory ahead. And when we walk in victory, it is Jesus who we see is ahead of us. Therefore, in this might, we should also determine to crush the head of the evil one. For when we walk hand in hand with each other, and with the Victor, we can hear the victory bells ringing even in heaven. And in unity, we shall enter His gates with thanksgiving. How can we forget victory: *For the weapons of our warfare are not carnal, but mighty through God to the pulling down strong* holds (2 Corinthians 10:4)?

# Come With Me

There is a deep down hunger in all of us to live forever. When all the hustle and bustle of this life is over, we want to go to a place where we can have peace - a place of splendor and full of joy. If this is our desire, then there ought to be such a place. This desire is not only universal but is the greatest and has always impacted mankind. Surely, our mind is not thinking it in vain since everyone ever living in this world has thought of it. Since it is so, is it that this desire could have come from God Almighty? If God had indeed implanted this idea in our hearts and mind, then there must be such a tranquil place of our longing.

Flying, we know what it is. It is leaving one destination and landing at another - it may be another city or country. But our taking off from one place to another is not complete until we had landed safely. However, we get on the plane trusting it will definitely land safely.

Flying often is exciting when we venture to new places. But going to a place called Paradise, of which everyone talks about, gives us goose bumps for it is a place where one can have perfect peace and can enjoy every moment. If it is a place of our dreams, it definitely is the answer to our quest. Just imagine being there and everyone so happy, flowers blooming, and the melody of the flowing waters making it breath taking. And landing there will make one forget all that the present busy life offers.

However, no one gets on any plane till they know where they are going and have full confidence that they will have a safe landing. There is a trip that we all have to take – *it is appointed unto men once to die* (Hebrews 9:27). But, no one knows when it is going to take place. Since this is the last trip, we all must be prepared it for it must not leave us wandering. For how many years or days we have lived on earth, when the time comes, it surprises everyone. However, there is a sure provision provided for us not to panic when it happens.

A VISA is required for travelling abroad. It provides a welcome reception for entering a country. Should it happen that we know somebody travelling with us who is from the country of our destination, the trip becomes more interesting because he lives there and knows all about that land. It becomes a sheer pleasure to travel with him. A VISA is also a Very Important Simple Answer.

There is a person who knows that place of our final destination because he came from there. He is greatly admired all over. He helped this dying man who was condemned to die on the cross. Just before he died, he talked to the other man who was also on His cross. His name was Jesus. Looking at Jesus, though dying, awe came upon him and he was sure that this was the man who could escort him where he will have peace. In the hearing of all who stood there, he said to Him: *Lord, remember me when thou comest into thy kingdom.* Immediately, the answer came back: *To day shalt thou be with me in paradise* (Luke 23:42-43). PARADISE? That's the place where I want to go?

Surely Jesus came to this earth to tell us all about this place and the Kingdom, and also how to get there. He accompanied this dying man that very night to this place. Yes, this is that place we all wish to go. Jesus died with the dying man in order to take him to this place though it cost Him His own life. This all took place in the open air and in the hearing of all who were present. And when Jesus died, the world witnessed His death. But on the third day He rose from the dead. He was alive. Many saw Him alive and well again. And He lives for evermore, and so does this man live with Him in His kingdom.

It was Jesus who accompanied this man on his last trip. He is not only the King there but is God Almighty. He wants to accompany us too when the time comes. He simply says, *come unto me* (Matthew 11:28) for: *I am the way, the truth and the life* (John 14:6).

In silence, the man on the cross is still saying 'come with me. Jesus by His resurrection has opened the way to Paradise for us all.' Like this man, believing that Jesus died for us too and will accompany us to our eternal home, He called, Paradise. This is that tranquil place where we can live ever happily. It is the place we have dreamed so long. To fulfill this great dream, it requires no theology, but just a simple sincere talk with Him, like

> Jesus, You died on the cross and I know you shed your blood there for me that I too could go with You to this place of my dreams. I confess many wrong things I have done and ask you to forgive me. Like this man, I do want to travel with You, dear Jesus, on my last journey. I would be delighted to tell others of You. Amen.

Jesus gave the Great Commission to His disciples at His resurrection, and poured out His heart for the world. For when He had seen the people in sin sitting under the shadow of death, He came to save them. Therefore, He also healed all those who were sick and wrapped them in His love. He united them to Himself and His wish was that they might likewise love one another and be united to Him. He delivered them from all physical and spiritual ailments. It was as if He was saying: Come with me on the wings of the morning to the place you have longed for.

Since we know that life beyond death is real, the possibility of existence of miracles and healing is still much debated. Many churches have been struggling with this question for so long. A dialogue should clarify this dilemma.

| | |
|---|---|
| Question: | Miracles and healing, are you real as the Bible says? For we have heard many say these are not for our times. |
| Answer: | I have been with you, how long you don't know I am with you, in you and around you, just see, I am so real. For without me you cannot live, and neither will there be life anywhere. |
| Question: | If you are real, why we do not see them? I am living my life and have all that I need. The world is at my finger tips and all I need my hands have provided. |

Answer:         The world that you live is a miracle of God – God made it;
The breath you breathe is the breath of God that
Adam received;
Miracles and healing are at work in each one, as
it started when the worlds were made
For miracles do take place when there is nothing
and unseen becomes visible.

The miracle of life starts at conception and reality becomes real in the womb;
The child though yet unborn, grows unseen, becomes delight of parents all lifelong.
The blood circulates and breath fills the lungs, God's hand has indeed been upon us.
The baby eats food God has made and body grows, God is in sight.

Water, the air, earth, sky and seas, all say, thank you God making us precious
And the cry of the child says: thank you for making me so comfortable and beautiful.
Yet the Bible says, there is a world beyond our present one for those who understand and believe
That for life beyond, Jesus has prepared a home in glory for believing in Him and life forever more.

On this earth, in compassion, Jesus is still calling sinners and sick to redeem them and heal them. Therefore, by faith in Christ Jesus the sick still are healed, the lame walk, the blind see and the dead are raised to life.

Jesus, who is real and so loving, commands us to do the works that He did – He went everywhere, He evangelized and He healed all manner of diseases.

Unity among the brethren was most in His mind when Jesus said: *That they all may be one.* The Bible boldly states: *Behold, how good and how pleasant it is for brethren to dwell together in unity* (Psalm 133:1). Jesus has commanded us to love one another. Surely in trusting and obeying Him, we *can do all things through Christ which strengthens me* (us) (Philippians 4:13). Therefore, should we not let His power and virtue so flow and shine for it will enable us to walk in His love and love each other as He has loved us? Because He is always with us, surely unity will become reality among us with His help and it will bring great joy among all the brethren irrespective of creed, color or denomination. It is all possible for God who holds the universe holds us too. This was the main reason that He has joined us to Himself on His Cross.

Jesus in His great love has desired so much for the unity in the body of His Church that not only He gave His life on the cross, but has given His glory for her too. For He has said: *And the glory which thou gavest me I have given them; that they may be one, even as we are one* (John 17:22).

# *The Light*

Genesis 1:1 states: *In the beginning God created the heavens and the earth*. Then God said : *Let there be light: and there was light*(Genesis 1:3).

It was in this light that the whole cosmos came into being, and it was God who created it. There was life in this light. Therefore, the whole universe became alive and bubbled in extraordinary delight, and in a song and perfect harmony shined with this bright light - and the entire cosmos was in view. In it were things seen and things unseen. There was life on the earth and in the seas fish and all life had flourished. While the earth was filled with life everywhere, in the sky and on the earth all creatures were seen. The last thing God created was mankind, which was the delight of God, for God created them in His own image.

In this light the universe was so lit that light flashed through the whole cosmos. Galaxies after galaxies appeared rejoicing and praising their Creator. They were all amazed to see such a mighty display of God's power for it was an extraordinary accomplishment that ever was displayed, and it covered this awesome universe. The earth could not contain her joy, and the whole cosmos danced, and still dances, in this glorious display of light with unspeakable joy.

With the march of time, this LIGHT marched into this world in the person of Jesus Christ, who is called 'Son of God' and who made it clear to all mankind by saying: *I am the light of the world* (John 8:12). He stated this because mankind had forgotten their Creator. *More over,* He also said: *I have come that they may have life, and that they may have it more abundantly"* (John 10:10).

We live in this world where there is abundance of life. But, if there is a more abundant life, we need to discover it for it too is manifested by this God given light.

## LIGHT

We know what light is. We have candlelight, gas light, electric light and there are many other sources of light. We also have the sun light and light from the stars and galaxies. On earth, the sunlight is the brightest and is most useful for life. The Bible tells us that there is much more provision yet available for meeting many life's needs, our present needs are as urgent for they prepare us for tomorrow. For example, deliverance of all mankind, salvation and eternal life are some of the attributes of this light. While it also has power over all sicknesses, ails and life's many struggles, virtue flows from this light graciously. There is no physical or spiritual need that it cannot meet. In it we find peace, joy that lasts a lifetime and makes life worth living in the midst of many of our trials and tribulations on this earth.

This light also reaches the recesses we have not known. It has power to heal the broken-hearted, has control over past, present and future, all life in heaven and earth, and also can transform people into the *'children of light'* (John 12:36). This light became flesh and dwelt among us. For when Jesus came to this earth in flesh, He said: *"I am the light of the world"* (John 8:12). This is that light that has created the whole universe we live in.

However, the word 'light' in the English language is often misunderstood. Or, should we say, that the English language should have another brighter word for such a magnificent and powerful light. There are many foreign languages that have words to describe such a great light, and there is definitely a great need for such a stronger word to describe this light. In the Urdu language, for example discover the word 'NOOR' which probably is more appropriate here because this light is greater than the sun's light or any other that we know. For example -

In Acts 26:13 we read Paul saying: *"At midday, O king, I saw in the way a light from heaven, above the brightness of the sun, shining round about me and them which journeyed with me"*. Since it was a brighter light than that of sun, we ought to call it with a better word than 'light'.

Jesus had said: *I am the light of the world* (John 8:12). This light apostle John described as 'noor' for having seen the glory of God, he wrote: *In him was life; and the life was the light of men. And the light shineth in darkness; and the darkness comprehended it not* (John 1:4-5). This light was seen by Paul on his way to Damascus - a light brighter than the sun, converting a sinner to be an apostle. This (noor) light is brighter than that we know. It is invisible too and also visible, lightening even the cosmos. This light was also seen by three disciples on the Mount of Transfiguration; for to see this light, even Moses and Elijah came, as the ancient and the present were soaked in *"noor"* enlightening them all.

## THE CANDLE

This light also can penetrate in our heart and life, for the Bible says: *For thou wilt light my candle: the Lord my God will enlighten my darkness* (Psalm 18:28). The light (*noor*) that shined from Jesus on the Mountain of Transfiguration is the *"noor"* that alone can lighten our heart, mind and soul.

This *"noor"* is so great and gentle that it changes even our heart and makes us also to shine with *"noor"* before others in this world. For when this *"noor"* comes and enlightens the candle of our heart, we have the light of God, or God living in us. With such great light in us, we have the power of God to move the mountains. Jesus has said: *"for without me ye can do nothing"* (John 15:5).

The Apostle John says: *That they all may be one; as thou, Father, art in me, and I in thee, that they also may be one in us: that the world may believe that thou hast sent me. And the glory which thou gavest me I have given them; that they may be one, even as we are one* (John 17:21-22). Jesus is saying:

I am in the Father and the Father in me and you in Me. Jesus, the light (*"noor"*) of the world, was therefore, made flesh and dwells in us; and thus, has made us: *the children of light* (John 12:36), the children of *"noor"*.

No one has the capability to lighten this candle in our heart. Jesus only, who has enlightened the whole universe, can light it, for our life is as precious to Him as the universe. He alone has the capability of emitting this light and wants us to lighten the world and to share the knowledge of His kingdom with others those around us. For He has said: *Let your light so shine before men that they may see your good works, and glorify your Father which is in heaven.* (Matthew 5:16).

Now He wants us to do something – just let His light shine that is in us. When we do this, we are imparting eternal life also, for we are letting *"noor"* to shine on others. Then when the world sees us doing so, the glory of God dawns upon this thirsty world. For in this light (*noor*), salvation takes us to the feet of Jesus, our author and *"noor"*. Then all the glory goes to Jesus who is the King of glory and the Church on earth is magnified. Jesus only is the *"noor"* of this world.

Now He commands us, the children of light (*noor*), to do the works that Jesus did: *Go into all the world* (Mark 16:15) and also says: *lo, I am with you always* (Matthew 28:20); and tell them that JESUS IS THE LIGHT OF THE WORLD. Thus, we let glory that He has given us shine that they (the world) see our good works (telling others of Jesus) and glorify the Father who is in heaven.

Let '*noor*' therefore so shine in the whole world that even the whole cosmos may shine brighter to see God's kingdom. For even the darkness will display light and the heavens will also display His praises.

# A Contemplation on the Lord's Pray

**Our Father which art in heaven, Hallowed be thy name.**
(Matthew 6:9) -

## OUR FATHER

Jesus taught this prayer to those who followed Him when He was on this earth. The first words He taught were: "Our Father". When we say, our Father, we declare that we all are one family. In this family are all those who ever lived and those who are living for they have dared to call Him, Our Father. Because God is our Father, His followers are His children and are brothers and sisters among ourselves. Because His blood that was shed for us, we are also endowed with His power, authority and glory.

## WHICH ART IN HEAVEN

Jesus had said: *where I am, there ye may be also* (John 14:3). Because God is our Father, He delights to take us to heaven also where His throne is. The Apostle John explains in Revelation 4:1: *I looked, and behold, a door was opened in heaven, and the first voice which I heard ... said, 'Come up hither'*. In verse 2, he says: *immediately I was in the spirit*. Likewise, we are escorted to heaven in the spirit and find ourselves standing before our God.

## HALLOWED BE THY NAME

If we are in the presence of a king, we greet that person as, Your Majesty, or Your Excellency in the presence of an ambassador, and so on. But meeting the Almighty God, the maker of heaven and earth, we do not know how to greet. Therefore, in awe we simply say: *Hallowed be thy Name.*

In the spirit and in the presence of our God, we instantly see the whole heaven open. (God also showed to Moses the whole promise land from Mount Pisgah.) There we behold the reign of God and perfect peace which is beyond any of our expectation. And there is a banquet table furnished for us to partake of it too.

**Thy kingdom come. Thy will be done in earth, as it is in heaven.** (Matthew 6:10) --

## THY KINGDOM COME

Visiting heaven and seeing tranquility and love prevailing, our spirit is stirred so much that we earnestly desire the same to prevail on this earth. We have been marred with cares and greed of this earth so much that only God's kingdom can make a difference.

## THY WILL BE DONE IN EARTH, AS IT IS IN HEAVEN

After visiting heaven, and being back to earth, how earnestly we desire that the same environment would prevail here also on the earth. Our understanding and eyes having been opened, though we are there just for a moment, we groan in the spirit that His will be done in earth also for now we know that the dwellers of this earth really need His reign desperately.

**Give us this day our daily bread.** (Matthew 6:11) -

## GIVE US THIS DAY OUR DAILY BREAD

When we were visiting heaven, we had tasted the delicacy of the table which was laid for us. It was food indeed. The Bible says that: *Every good gift and every perfect gift is from above, and cometh down from the Father of lights* (James 1:17). The children of Israel were blessed in the wilderness for they ate the bread that came down from heaven. Jesus came to this earth to feed us this bread. He is the bread of Life. For He said: *I am the living bread which came down from heaven: if any man eat of this bread, he shall live* (John 6:51). And: *Whoso eateth my flesh, and drinketh my blood, hath eternal life ... For my flesh is meat indeed, and my blood is drink indeed* (John 6:54,55). This was the bread that we ate in heaven and are back on earth when we study the Word of God in our Bible study. In such times, the Holy Spirit opens the doors of love and grace and strengthens our mind, and brings to our memory all that Jesus had said. Sitting at the feet of Jesus, led by the Holy Spirit, and in our Father's presence, His blessings come to us soaking us with His love divine. Then we see for ourselves that the table He has furnished for us is really gorgeous.

**And forgive us our debts, as we forgive our debtors.** (Matthew 6:12) -

## AND FORGIVE US OUR DEBTS

The Prophet Isaiah was an anointed prophet. But having seen a vision, he said: *Woe is me! for I am undone; because I am a man of unclean lips* (Isaiah 6:5). If Isaiah considered himself of unclean lips: *we all have come short of the glory of God* (Romans 3:26). We too need to repent of all our sins, endeavors, dogmas and creeds that have made a schism in the body of Christ. We need to approach the throne of Grace in awe.

## AS WE FORGIVE OUR DEBTORS

When we ask Jesus to forgive our trespasses, we are standing in His presence before the throne of Grace. It is a very holy moment and action. However God requires that we forgive all who have trespassed, and also those who have not trespassed against us. For Jesus had expressly said: *if ye forgive not men their trespasses, neither will your Father forgive your trespasses* (Matthew 6:15). Jesus forgave those who hated and killed Him. This love of Jesus constrains us to forgive all irrespective of who they are. This is the demand of true love. Was it not that Jesus said: *This is my commandment, That ye love one another, as I have loved you* (John 15:12)?

When we delight to forgive others, loving them will take us to a higher plane of knowing God's immeasurable love. Then to share Jesus with the lost humanity, which has been laden with 'not forgiving', will bring many to the Kingdom of our God.

**And lead us not into temptation, but deliver us from evil: For thine is the kingdom and the power, and the glory, for ever. Amen.** (Matthew 6:13) -

## AND LEAD US NOT INTO TEMPTATION

Our adversary the devil is still on this earth. He surely tempts us and will tempt us still. He tested Jesus till the end, will he leave us alone? Since Jesus said: *lo, I am with you always* (Matthew 28:20), it is our joy that we have a friend in Jesus, all our sins and grieves to bear. He never fails to rescue whenever we call for His help.

## BUT DELIVER US FROM EVIL

Jesus alone has the power to save and to deliver us from all attacks of the enemy. He rescued the dying man on the cross who called on Him, and took him to Paradise Himself. He is the Way when there is no other way. Has He not said: *I am the way, the truth and the life* (John 14:6)? He delivers us not only from sins but all sicknesses, demonic world and all the works of the enemy in physical and spiritual realms, even things which are unknown to us in the spiritual worlds.

## FOR THINE IS THE KINGDOM, AND THE POWER, AND THE GLORY, FOR EVER

In the kingdom of our Father, there is joy unspeakable and full of glory. The universe displays His power in all things, seen and unseen. He holds the whole universe. His power is infinite indeed. For those who are in His Kingdom, the Bible says: *And they that be wise shall shine as the brightness of the firmament; and they that turn many to righteousness as the stars for ever and ever* (Daniel 12:3). Great honor is bestowed upon those who are His.

On earth He delivers us from all works of darkness and tells us that we are His children. It was not enough for Him to make us His children; He made us children of resurrection too. It was still not enough, for in His infinite love He gave us his glory also that we might love each other as He did.

In His kingdom His glory has no end. This glory is shared by all who are His on this earth and in heaven. Because we are His children, He has also given us the power and authority to fight against all that the devil has on earth and in heavenly places. *For we wrestle not against flesh and blood, but again principalities, against powers, against the rulers of the darkness of this world, against spiritual wickedness in high places* (Ephesians 6:12). It is sheer love that the glory that was His alone, He gave us freely. This is the glory the Apostle Paul desired that we all might be saturated in it and be changed from glory to glory.

## AMEN

When we say AMEN, our desire becomes to do His will and desires. Was it not the desire of our Lord Jesus Christ: *That they all may be one, as thou, Father, art in me, and I in thee, that they also may be one in us* (John 17:21)? Therefore, by saying this prayer, we affix our spiritual signature by saying: our FATHER we all are one with You and one in the family of God.

CPSIA information can be obtained
at www.ICGtesting.com
Printed in the USA
LVHW031138240322
714287LV00009B/641